Bloom County
BABYLON
FIVE YEARS OF BASIC NAUGHTINESS

Bloom County Books by Berke Breathed

LOOSE TAILS
'TOONS FOR OUR TIMES
PENGUIN DREAMS and Stranger Things
BLOOM COUNTY BABYLON: Five Years of Basic Naughtiness

BERKE BREATHED

Bloom County
BABYLON
FIVE YEARS OF BASIC NAUGHTINESS

LITTLE, BROWN AND COMPANY

BOSTON   TORONTO

FIRST EDITION

Some of the cartoon strips in this book were previously published in
Bloom County: "Loose Tails" (1983), *'Toons for Our Times: A Bloom
County Book* (1984), and *Penguin Dreams and Stranger Things* (1985).

BLOOM COUNTY is syndicated by The Washington Post Writers Group.

Library of Congress Cataloging-in-Publication Data
Breathed, Berke.
  Bloom County Babylon.
  "A Bloom County book."
  Selections from the author's comic strip, Bloom
County.
  I. Title.
PN6728.B57B68   1986   741.5′973   86-14772
ISBN 0-316-10724-7
ISBN 0-316-10309-8 (pbk.)

WAK

*Published simultaneously in Canada
by Little, Brown & Company (Canada) Limited*

PRINTED IN THE UNITED STATES OF AMERICA

To Sophie,
my love, my life, my dog

"I have often had the impression that, to penguins, man is just another penguin—different, less predictable, occasionally violent, but tolerable company when he sits still and minds his own business."

—*Bernard Stonehouse*

"JOIN ME IN THE HILLS!" he yelled in passing. "ONLY THE PROPERLY EQUIPPED WILL SURVIVE!"
His fatigues were freshly pressed.

The Great LaRouche Toad-Frog Massacree

by Michael J. Binkley

Adapted from *Daze of My Youth: A Bloom County Memoir*,
published by Little, Brown and Co.

THE SUMMER OF 1988 DESCENDED on Bloom County much as it had for each of the previous nine years of my life; humid and without hint of the chaos ahead. We needed no hints, however, for calamity always rode shotgun with Bloom County summers. Each spring, bored boys awaited the hot months with the giddy anticipation normally reserved for the imminent approach of a gang of Nazi motorcyclists. Things were going to *happen*. Wonderful things. Catastrophic things. And if that meant, say, that my dad's new Chrysler LeBaron were to be dynamited by Japanese antiprotectionist guerrillas, so be it. This was summer, after all, and such things simply happen. Confident in the knowledge that soon the June sun would fry most of the common sense out of everyone's noodle, Milo and I would kick back among the meadow dandelions and wait for things to generally fall apart. As I said, this summer was to be no different.

These were contented times for me, being, at age ten, still safely ignorant of what my adulthood would bring (namely, a clerkship at the lingerie counter of Wal-mart, a job that would send some fetishists I know into palm-sweating ecstasy but which, alas, still sends me to my knees with nausea. See chapter 11, "Women and Nausea"). These were, in fact, generally contented times for everyone. A presidential election was approaching, but it would be another four years before Clint Eastwood reached the White House and really stirred things up, so for the moment, life was pretty tranquil. This, I figure, helps explain the exaggerated behavior of Bloom Countians over what happened that summer.

The Great LaRouche Toad-Frog Massacree, as it became known, had its roots in two entirely separate and unrelated events: a conspiracy of happenstance which was to test the civil defense preparedness of an entire American community and forever alter the ecological food chain of the North Meadow Pond.

On June 21, 1988, the following item appeared on page 3 of the daily *Bloom Beacon,* sandwiched between an article on the plummeting price of cow tongue and "Dear Abby":

COMMUNISTS AT U.S. DOORSTEP

by Milo Bloom, Investigative Reporter

Today it was discovered that after years of aggressive expansion, the Soviet Union has stretched its borders to within a mere 12 miles of American soil. The State Department has no immediate comment.

...which wasn't particularly surprising since the State Department had been aware for some time that the easternmost tip of Siberia comes within a polar bear's whisker of Alaska, but who cares since it's too damned cold to worry about. But the vast bulk of the *Beacon's* readership had no such knowledge and a subdued rumble of patriotic consternation coursed through the local population like some frightening new flu virus. The consensus was that something ought to be done. "SOMETHING," bellowed Steve Dallas at a hastily called town meeting, "SHOULD BE DONE!" He pounded the table, looking properly drunk with nationalistic fervor. Eunice Annanburg suggested CIA assassinations of most of the Kremlin, but she was soundly overruled in favor of a more moderate response. A letter would be dispatched to the President informing him of the crisis. (Years later, Caspar Weinberger would write in his memoirs that he had been sent to the White House to reassure Mr. Reagan that it wasn't necessary to send the Sixth

Fleet to investigate this new business. We were pleased our letter had attracted the attention it deserved. The President was a fave-rave in Bloom County.)

A high level of media-inspired hysteria and paranoia having now been generated, the stage was set for the second minor incident to complete the general breakdown of order that led to The Great LaRouche Toad-Frog Massacree. And it happened early the next Sunday morning, deep within the Bloom County Volunteer Fire Department's wiring system. Several errant electrons jumped when they shouldn't have at a place they shouldn't have, resulting in what shouldn't have happened. In short, a short. The air-raid siren came to life for the first time in Bloom County history.

It must have started about 6:00 in the morning and, it being Sunday, caught everyone asleep. At least everyone in Milo's boardinghouse, where my father and I lived. Bolting upright in bed, eyes wide, I listened to the wail outside and knew immediately that this day was to be dealt a perfectly proper dose of pandemonium. The Nazi motorcyclists had, so to speak, arrived. A nuclear missile attack was not safe but it was certainly *not* boring.

"Get under the door frames!" yelled Dad, huddling beneath his as I emerged from my room. I told Dad that standing under door frames was usually something done during an earthquake and that he might have been mixing up his catastrophes—but by then the rest of the residents had emerged and were milling around the top of the staircase, listening to the siren and peering up at the ceiling. These, I later thought, are the many foolish things people do while waiting for Russian missiles.

Standing there in our various forms of undress, nobody had to say what we were all thinking. That newly discovered twelve-mile gap between our peace-loving people and the Soviet hordes had been just too tempting and the Bolsheviks had decided to get the jump on us. "I *TOLD* you all that something should have been done!" said Steve Dallas, who was pounding the wall wearing only Fruit of the Loom briefs. That Steve also was barefoot was actually the greatest danger we faced at the moment, his feet being considered a public health hazard within a five-county area. In Bloom County, prolonged bachelorhood is often looked at with suspicion, but in Steve's case it was merely a consequence of poor foot hygiene: women were simply never seen in his company. Now, Steve didn't look much like what a homosexual was generally presumed to look like, so folks accepted the foot theory and gave him little trouble as long as he kept his loafers on. Normally, aging bachelors can be a real moral strain on a small town.

The siren still screamed and Milo quickly took control of the situation. "Okay!" he said, "Where's our Civil Defense Coordinator?" This was a good question, since Opus, who held that office, was missing. . . . A quick search found him sitting on the pot with the Sunday funnies. A late night of questionable activities had apparently taken their toll, for he was asleep with the comics draped over him like a quilt. Our Civil Defense Coordinator was awakened rudely and dragged, struggling in a half nelson, to the top of the stairs.

I should digress to explain that the more unsavory positions of official authority within the boardinghouse bureaucracy were given to those members who made the unfortunate mistake of being absent for house meetings. Thus Opus, much to his eventual horror, had been given the honor of being voted Official Trash Coordinator, Official Wasp Nest Remover, Official Rain Gutter Cleaner, Official Chimneysweep, and Official Handler of Steve Dallas's Socks—positions he earned by being off somewhere in Milo's Meadow picking his nose when the nominations were made. These were underhanded actions and complaints were lodged. But this—this Official Civil Defense Coordinator business was something altogether different. That awful Sunday morning in June was the first Opus had heard about this new office. "ME?" he cried. "ME? Nope! No way. No no no! Uh-uh! ME?" He started to hyperventilate, so we wiped his brow with a cool rag and got him some herring entrails and grape juice, which calmed him down some.

With the collapse of the only official leadership, the situation began to deteriorate. Thermonuclear bombs were due at any moment, things had to be done. Panic had to be averted. Steve realized what he needed to do and returned to his room while the rest of us regrouped outside in the street. Opus, dazed and faint with anxiety, was propped up and federal civil defense instructions were shoved into his hands. Dad, Milo, his grandfather, Oliver Wendell Jones and his parents from next door, passersby in the street, all came to attention and awaited instructions. The sirens wailed on. Obviously only minutes remained.

"'First,'" said Opus, reading from the government manual, "'Gather shovels.'" We dispersed and looked for shovels, returning with several. "'Second, quickly and without panic, take refuge in countryside.'" Shovels in hand, we formed an orderly line and proceeded to march behind our hyperventilating leader down the street, passing by others who were clearly reacting to the threat of thermonuclear annihilation with less self-control than ourselves. We, after all, had taken the precaution of procuring not only an official federal civil defense handbook, but an official—if reluctant—Civil Defense Coordinator as well.

Upon reaching the dandelions of Milo's Meadow, well removed, we supposed, from Ground Zero, we stood at attention and awaited further instructions. *"'Dig shallow trenches,'"* Opus continued. *"'Lie down in trenches, cover self with wooden door or like object and await blast. After shock wave passes, emerge and go to nearest emergency Civil Defense Center and fill out emergency change of address forms.'"*

With this, we seized the handbook and hacked it to pieces with our shovels. Opus was officially decommissioned and we quickly adopted a favorite stand-by approach to an approaching holocaust—hysterical panic. This is always fun to watch, so Milo and I settled back into the grass to savor the confusion, our own fates apparently sealed. Opus wrung his hands and worried about what radiation would do to his complexion.

Steve Dallas jogged by, dressed in designer fatigues and wearing an extraordinarily full backpack. "JOIN ME IN THE HILLS!" he yelled in passing. "ONLY THE PROPERLY EQUIPPED WILL SURVIVE!" Or the lawyers, we thought. "JOIN ME AND WE'LL CRAWL FROM THE RUBBLE AND LIVE TO FIGHT ANOTHER DAY. TO THE HILLS! ONLY THE WEAK WILL PERISH!" This was no comfort to a nearly shattered Opus, who had no illusions as to where he stood in the strong/weak classification. Watching his best friend Steve Dallas disappear into the woods dressed like Rambo proved the final decisive blow to an already critical frame of mind and he plopped over unconscious. Lying serenely among the clover, Opus was blessedly unaware of Portnoy and Hodge-Podge marching up the hill with a fully automatic 45mm American Ruger Assault rifle, apparently intent upon massacring the imminent hordes of Communists in groups of fifty or more. "We're gonna massacree 'em!" bellowed Portnoy, waving the weapon that had obviously been recently borrowed from the shelves of the K-Mart Sporting Goods Section. Milo and I, concluding that the general scheme of things just couldn't handle *this* much fun, tried to dissuade Portnoy and his fellow conspirator from their patriotic mission. They would not hear of it. These, after all, were a groundhog and a rabbit, two of the most excitable critters to be found in modern meadows and wont to excessive behavior. "We'll go out blasting!" they said.

Down we went, following these two warriors, to the North Meadow Pond, where invading Russians were suspected. Opus awoke and trailed this dangerous procession, rubbing his stomach, for nuclear war had upset it. If he was to die in a fireball, he thought, it would be nice to go to Heaven without gas. This was obviously not to be and the crushing reality pushed him further into a deep funk. He was nearly to the point of tears when Portnoy, aiming into the water of the North Meadow Pond where the Communists were hiding in their scuba equipment, pulled the trigger of his massacre machine. "I CAN SEE THEIR EYES! YAAAAAAA!" he screamed, or something like that. For a full minute, automatic weapon fire tore into the little pond, turning it into a horrible, savage, boiling

froth of hot lead and foam. We hit the ground as the spray of bullets continued, tearing up trees, rocks, sod, an old inner tube—oh, it was simply horrific. Order was restored when the ammo was exhausted and we picked ourselves off the ground. Opus had, at the first blast, collapsed in cardiac arrest and was briefly thought to be shot, but after thorough and prolonged CPR, was brought back to full consciousness, walking away from the incident with only minor emotional troubles.

Back at the battle scene, we survivors checked for bullet holes in our clothing. Portnoy sat on his rump, the gun on his lap smoking. He surveyed the sight in front of him and quietly exhaled a low, sliding whistle, much as one might do when passing a terrible car wreck.

There, floating facedown in the turbid water, were hundreds, no, *thousands* of corpses...legs wide apart, arms spread, tongues extended their full eight or ten inches. It was plain as pie that there wasn't a single living toad-frog remaining in that pond. The overwhelming magnitude of the crime grew on us as we stood around, eyes bulging and mouths agape. "Look at Portnoy," I whispered to Milo, for indeed, the crushing realization of guilt at what he'd done came across his face like a shadow, and he slumped in shame. These tragic victims were clearly not Russians, although he could have sworn they *were* when he first saw their gleaming eyes in the early morning light.

Milo, realizing that Portnoy's emotional stability was at stake, went to his side and explained that while, admittedly, the likelihood of those toad-frogs being Communists, or even liberals, was not great, there was no reason to assume that he had wiped out supply-side Republicans instead. In fact, there was an excellent chance that the vast majority of them were LaRouche Democrats, who, of course, were better off dead.

This revelation appeared to cheer Portnoy, and the entire party headed back into town where we stopped off for Egg McMuffins, the air-raid siren having long since been silenced and the general domestic tranquillity restored. The newspapers recorded Portnoy's excesses that pandemonious day as The Great LaRouche Toad-Frog Massacree, an honor which won him some brief celebrity and a quick appearance, via satellite, on "Nightline." Things settled down soon afterward and, except for the frequency of fried LaRouche frogs' legs served at supper, normalcy returned to haunt the remaining summer.

I neglected to mention, however, that Steve Dallas was eventually discovered by a small and unenthusiastic search team several days after the Massacree, lying spread-eagled and dazed among the summer hyacinths and surrounded by the remnants of his survivalist base camp, now in a state of higgledy-piggledly. A blow-dryer, blender, toaster, piña colada mix, microwave oven, and other essentials of survival lay scattered among the barbed wire and camouflage netting. His formerly impressive fatigues were nowhere to be seen. The shocking truth is that all he was wearing was an argyle sock and a bad sunburn. Opus bent down and put an ear to Steve's mouth just in time to hear him whisper, "The horror...the horror...I...forgot...the...mayonnaise." We took him home and rubbed Noxzema all over him and put him to bed, where he remained for the better part of the week stuck to the sheets.

16

ADOLESCENCE IS SNEAKING UP ON YOU FAST-LIKE, MILO OL'BOY... THERE'S SOME BASIC DECISIONS TO BE MADE.

MANHOOD IS A SERIOUS BUSINESS... WITH SERIOUS QUESTIONS TO APPROACH...

AND, INDEED, ONE DAY, I, MILO BLOOM, MAY FIND THE ANSWER TO THE PROVERBIAL QUESTION THAT ALL GOOD MEN MUST ASK THEMSELVES...

ARE A PAIR OF "FRUIT OF THE LOOM" BRIEFS AS SEXY AS WE THINK?

IS THAT **YOU** RACHEL? I HAVEN'T SEEN YOU FOR MONTHS!

ISABEL HONEY! YOU'RE LOOKING CUTE AS EVER.

MY LANDS... I JUST **LOVE** YOUR HAIR... YOU'RE SO BEAUTIFUL I COULD JUST KILL YOU.

AND **YOU!** SO THIN I COULD SIMPLY SCREAM... I'LL JUST **HAVE** TO LEARN YOUR SECRET...

HMM...

MMM...

BEEN BLEACHING THOSE ROOTS LATELY, RACHEL?

EAT DEATH YOU OVER WEIGHT LITTLE TART.

OK. HERE WE GO... THIS IS THE STORY OF SNOW WHITE AND THE SEVEN DWARFS...

HOLD IT.

BACK UP.

SO WHAT'S WRONG WITH SNOW WHITE AND THE SEVEN DWARFS?

SNOW WHITE. ALWAYS SNOW WHITE. THERE'S OTHER COLORS YA' KNOW DEAR BOY.

AND THIS DWARF BUSINESS. SHORT PEOPLE DESERVE BETTER THAN THIS NONSENSE.

AHEM...

THIS IS THE STORY OF PITCH BLACK AND THE SEVEN BIG HONKIES...

DANDY.

QUITE.

AHA. THERE SITS FREIDA HUNZUCKER. I KNOW WHAT'S ON HER MIND... JUST HOW NAIVE DOES THIS DAME THINK I AM?

OH MILO... YOU MAN OF MEN... YOU CHUNK OF VIRILE MASCU- LINITY...

YEP. THERE SHE GOES. LOSING COMPLETE CONTROL.

QUICK MILO... I CAN'T STAND IT... GIVE ME A SMOOCH!

OKAY, OKAY... JUST SIT DOWN AND I'LL GIVE YOU A SMOOCH.

I AM SITTING DOWN, AND YOU CAN JUST PUT A REIN ON THOSE LIPS, BUB.

OH YES... YES OF COURSE.

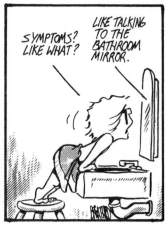

Do my hazel orbs deceive me? I am before a palace! A rural château! A veritable BUNGALOW OF BEAUTY!

BLOOM'S BOARDING HOUSE

And what have we here? A young nobleman no less! A junior proprietor of this establishment no doubt.

And myself... call me "LIMEKILLER"... a gallant globe-trotter forever in search of sustenance for the soul and cover from the elements.

You're a bum and you need a cheap room.

Such a wise knave you are. Lead on, Shorty.

This is Mr. Limekiller. He'd like to rent a room. I vote yes.

Well I don't. He looks like a bum to me.

Ah... chère madame, vos lobes d'oreilles sont comme têtes de poisson.

Oh my! That's French isn't it?

Oui, madame.

He stays.

Humph.

What'd you say?

Not sure... something like "your earlobes resemble fish heads."

Your room is at the end of the hall, Mr. Limekiller. You'll be sharing a bath with the widow Rubie Tucker...

AAIGH! WATCH IT, BOY!

Good heavens...

Keep your distance, you... you vagrant.

She's a little shy.

Shorty, there's no such thing as a SHY water buffalo.

Hi folks! Welcome to the home of Ronald McDonald and Mayor McCheese!

McDONALD'S

So what kind of McMunchies would you like? How about an EGG McMuffin? Or an all-beef McFeast? Or maybe our newest treat... CHICKEN McNuggets!

McYUMMY!

McDONALD'S

Let's get a McPIZZA.

McFINE with me.

McBREATHED

ELEANOR, WHAT ARE YOU DOING HERE?

NOW IS THAT ANY WAY TO GREET YOUR "EX" AFTER 3 YEARS, CHARLES, DEAR?

ESPECIALLY AFTER I'VE SPENT THE LAST 3 WEEKS TRACKING YOU DOWN TO THIS WILDERNESS OUT IN THE MIDDLE OF ABSOLUTELY NOWHERE....I MEAN REALLY, CHARLES, THIS IS SIMPLY THE STICKS.

AND I MUST SAY, DEAR...EVEN FOR YOU, THESE PEOPLE AROUND HERE ARE RATHER... WELL, HOW SHOULD I SAY IT...?

PROVINCIAL.

COMMON.

PEASANTS.

WELL, ELEANOR, AFTER 3 YEARS, I DON'T QUITE KNOW WHAT TO ASK... UH... WELL, HOW ARE THE KIDS?

LITTLE MICHAEL IS NOW A PUNK ROCKER WITH PURPLE HAIR, RICKY IS IN THE MILITARY ACADEMY RUNNING GUNS TO EL SALVADOR AND DEBRA JO IS ABOUT TO RUN OFF TO ITALY WITH HER ORTHODONTIST AND JOIN THE "RED BRIGADE."

HOW'S THE LAWN?

DEAD.

DEBRA JO? IS THAT YOU? YOUR MOTHER IS HERE AND, WELL... I JUST THOUGHT I'D GIVE YOU A CALL.

DADDY! IT'S BEEN SO LONG!

NOW LISTEN HONEY, YOUR MOTHER SAID THAT YOU QUIT YOUR SORORITY AND PLAN TO GO TO ITALY AND JOIN THE "RED BRIGADE."...

ISN'T IT EXCITING? LONG LIVE THE STRUGGLE!

YES...WELL, I JUST WANT YOU TO ALWAYS REMEMBER ONE THING, HONEY...

YES, DADDY?

TO ME, YOU'LL ALWAYS BE THE LITTLE GIRL IN THE PINK BUNNY SUIT.

OH DADDY! ALWAYS THE BOURGEOIS PIG!

BARTENDER, GIVE ME A BROKEN-HEARTED BOURBON OF BLEAKNESS... MIXED WITH A LITTLE TONIC OF DISMALNESS...

AND YOU CAN THROW IN A DASH OF CRÈME DE MISERY, WITH...WITH A TWIST OF DESPAIR...

...AND PUT IT ALL ON THE ROCKS OF WRETCHEDNESS

BONK!

EXCUSE ME, BUT COULD YOU PASS ME THE PEANUTS OF PATHOS?

CERTAINLY.

THE PLUCKY NEW SCHOOLTEACHER IN TOWN PAUSES...HER FIRST BIG CHALLENGE LYING BEFORE HER IN THIS WILDERNESS CALLED "BLOOM COUNTY."

SHE IS CALM...AS IS THE WIND BEFORE A STORM... FOR SHE BRINGS CULTURE, NEW IDEAS AND NOT JUST A LITTLE FEMINISM TO THIS LAST WILD AMERICAN FRONTIER...

HEY PA! TAKE A GANDER AT THIS LITTLE NUMBER!

THE NATIVES EMERGE TO GREET HER.
BOY! I SURE CAN PICK 'EM!
GOOD EYE, SON!

HELLO PEOPLE. I'M MS. BOBBI HARLOW...YOUR NEW GURU.
OH MISS HARLOW... ARE YOU WEIRD?

2 + 2
$E = MC^2$

WHAT?
MY PA SAID THAT "ANY DAME THAT ISN'T MARRIED BY THE AGE OF 21 IS EITHER UGLY OR WEIRD." THAT'S A QUOTE.

UGLY OR WEIRD? WHY THAT...THAT... OOOO...!

VOCABULARY TIME, FOLKS. WHAT'S THE DEFINITION OF "LIBERATED WOMAN?"
"A PLUCKED HEN." THAT'S ANOTHER QUOTE.

JUST LOOK AT OUR NEW FLOOZY TEACHER, BETSY. JUST WHO DOES THIS "MS. BOBBI HARLOW" THINK SHE IS, ANYHOW?
YEAH!

FRANKLY, I DON'T LIKE HER. YOU JUST CAN'T TRUST ATTRACTIVE WOMEN, BETSY... KNOW WHY?
WHY?

BECAUSE THEY MAKE ALL THE AVAILABLE MEN IN THE VICINITY ACT LIKE COMPLETE FATHEADS.

YOU FELLAS NEED ANYTHING IN PARTICULAR?
NOPE.
NOPE.
NOPE.
NOPE.
NOPE.

YES, MISTER..? MISTER..?
BLOOM. MILO BLOOM. THE BOYS AND I WROTE YOU A POEM. WE HOPE YOU'LL BE TOUCHED...

"WELCOME TO OUR CLASSROOM; WE'LL GROW TO LOVE YOU REAL SOON! TEACH US MATH AND SCIENCE AND PLATO; WE ALL THINK YOU'RE QUITE A... A..."

TOMATO.
"...TOMATO."

SIDDOWN!
SHE'S NOT TOUCHED.

Panel 1: OH MR. PIPKINS... I'M NOT SURE ABOUT OUR NEW FIFTH GRADE TEACHER... MISS HARLOW. SHE JUST DOESN'T SEEM... RIGHT.

Panel 2: NONSENSE, MISS BLATZ. SHE'S VERY DEDICATED. IN FACT, SHE'S EVEN INVITED A SPECIAL GUEST TO SPEAK TO HER CLASS TODAY.

Panel 3: OH THAT'S NICE... ON WHAT? / ENERGY, I THINK.

Panel 4: OK... WOW, CAN ALL YOU LITTLE DUDES SAY "NUCLEAR ANNIHILATION?" / NUGLIR ANILUSHUN. / NO NUKES

Panel 5: MISS HARLOW... A TEN YEAR OLD BOY JUST RAN BY MY OFFICE SCREAMING, "ANARCHY FOR THE '80'S!" NOW, I'D LIKE AN EXPLANATION.

Panel 6: BOO!

Panel 7: AND WHAT IS THE MEANING OF THIS?

Panel 8: IT'S IN CASE THE FISHES TEAR-GAS ME. / "FASCISTS," DEAR.

Panel 9: MAKE ME A CORNED BEEF SANDWICH, WOULD YOU, BESS? / WELL I'M NOT SURE I SHOULD, DEAR...

Panel 10: MS. HARLOW TOLD ME HOW SAD IT IS TO ALLOW MYSELF TO BE TREATED AS A MARITAL SLAVE. SHE SAID IT MERELY INDICATES A TRAGIC LACK OF LOVE DURING THE AUTUMN OF OUR LIVES.

Panel 11: OH BESS... I DO LOVE YOU, REALLY, I DO. / AND I LOVE YOU, DEAR.

Panel 12: GOOD. HOLD THE MAYO. / YES DEAR.

Panel 13: I DON'T WANT TO PLAY FOOTBALL. I HATE FOOTBALL. I WANT TO BE A COMPUTER PROGRAMMER. I HATE PAIN. I'M HAVING AN ANXIETY ATTACK...

Panel 14: AND YOUR GRANDFATHER BEING COACH THIS YEAR DOESN'T HELP, MILO... HE'S VERY PECULIAR, YA KNOW. / I KNOW.

Panel 15: JUST LOOKIT HIM UP THERE! HE WORRIES ME, MILO... HE REALLY DOES. / I KNOW...

Panel 16: MEN... FOOTBALL IS WAR. GOD, HOW I LOVE IT SO...

I'M BORED, STEVE. LIFE IS TOO SHORT TO BE BORED. I'M 25 AND MY BIG NIGHT CONSISTS OF A MOVIE, A BOX OF BON-BONS AND YOU.

TRY TO GRASP THIS...ENJOYING LIFE SHOULD BE DIPPING TOES IN A COUNTRY STREAM...COUNTING THE STARS...DOING CARTWHEELS IN THE PARK, CELEBRATING THE JOY OF LIFE BY BREATHING DEEP ITS BLISS!

OKAY. LET'S TRY THIS ON THE BON-BONS...

BREATHING BLISS?

TURN TO PAGE SIX, CLASS.

JUST A SECOND, MISS HARLOW. WE'D LIKE SOME ANSWERS ABOUT LAST NIGHT.

LAST NIGHT?

YES. YOU ASSOCIATED WITH A CERTAIN YOUNG MAN. YOU'RE ON, MILO...

SUBJECT: STEVE DALLAS
JOB: ATTORNEY
I.Q.: QUESTIONABLE
MORALS: QUESTIONABLE
COMMENTS: WEARS UNMATCHING, PASTEL-COLORED SOCKS.

I AM APPALLED!

FRANKLY, SO ARE WE.

HEAR! HEAR!

TAKE NOTES, CLASS... THE FIRST SLIDE IS "WOMAN IN FIELD", BY RENOIR; NEO-FRENCH IMPRESSIONISM.

THAT'S NO WOMAN IN A FIELD.

YOU'RE RIGHT. AND THIS IS HARDLY RENOIR; NEO-FRENCH IMPRESSIONISM...

I THINK I SEE THE PROBLEM. MAYBE THE NICE YOUNG MAN AT THE PROJECTOR WOULD LIKE TO TELL US WHAT WE'RE REALLY LOOKING AT.

"GIRL ON BEACH" BY STEVE DALLAS; NEO-FRENCH BIKINI.

HOW DO YOU SPELL THAT?

DAD...I KNOW HOW YOU THINK I'M A FAILURE AS A SON...MY BALLET AND ALL...BUT I'M GONNA TRY ONCE MORE. DAD, I GOT MYSELF A DOG.

I KNOW HOW YOU THINK EVERY NORMAL BOY SHOULD HAVE A DOG...SO I BOUGHT A GERMAN SHEPHERD...VERY MACHO! HERE BOY!

GREAT SCOTT. THAT'S A PENGUIN.

IT IS? OH DEAR.

MARGARET? I'M GOING TO TRADE OUR SON IN FOR A NEW SUBARU.

WHAT?

32

WELL, MOM...DAD...ENOUGH ABOUT **MY** PRIVATE LIFE. HOW'S THE OL' MARRIAGE?

OH JUST FINE, DEAR.

RIGHT. SO WHEN WAS THE LAST TIME YOU TWO SLEPT IN THE SAME BED TOGETHER?

OH... 1959.

WHAT?

WELL EVIDENTLY I SNORE LIKE A "CONGESTED HEIFER," DEAR.

DADDY!

"SNORT! SNORT!"

SURPRISE, BOBBI! YOUR PRINCE MACHO IS HERE!

OH NO... NOT NOW.

NOW LISTEN... MY FOLKS ARE HERE. YOU'RE GOING TO HAVE TO MEET THEM... SO FOR ONCE IN YOUR CREEPY LIFE, JUST TRY...**TRY** TO MAKE A GOOD IMPRESSION. PLEASE!

UM... MOTHER, I'D LIKE YOU TO MEET A... A FRIEND OF MINE. MISTER STEVE DALLAS.

BLEAH.

STEVE!

I DIDN'T SAY NOTHIN'!

THAT'S RIGHT, MISTER HARLOW... I GRADUATED LAST YEAR WITH A LAW DEGREE... BUT I'M INTO WHATEVER WILL MAKE ME FILTHY RICH.

THEN LISTEN CAREFULLY BOY...

ONE WORD. THERE'S ONLY **ONE WORD** FOR THE EIGHTIES, SON. JUST ONE WORD.

ONE WORD.

ONE WORD.

PLASTICS.

HANDGUNS. DISPOSABLE HANDGUNS.

SAY, LIMEKILLER... WHAT ARE PRINCE CHARLES AND DIANA UP TO LATELY?

ROYAL HONEYMOON. VERY SECRET LOCATION.

WHICH YOUR SOURCES SAY IS...?

NEW YORK CITY.

THE ROYAL TWOSOME IN **NEW YORK**?

CAN YOU JUST IMAGINE?

LOOK, CHAP... TURN THE BLOODY THING DOWN OR I'LL HAVE YOU HUNG BY YOUR TOES.

CHARLIE...

BUS STOP

34

PAPERWORK? YOU DO PAPERWORK? YA MEAN YOU'RE NOT EVEN A COOK? MY LITTLE FLOWER OF THE FONDUES IS JUST A FIGUREHEAD?

WELL... I...

AAIGH! I BARE MY HEART AND BETTY CROCKER SHISH KEBABS IT.

"SHISH KEBAB." IT'S A COOKING TERM.

OH.

WELL, KID, SORRY I DIDN'T MEET YOUR EXPECTATIONS.

YES...WELL, SOMETIMES WE DON'T LIKE TO SEE THINGS AS THEY REALLY ARE.

YA KNOW, I CAME LOOKING FOR THE REAL AMERICA IN BETTY CROCKER... AND KNOW WHAT? I THINK I'VE FOUND IT. FAREWELL.

OVERLY HYPED BUT BASICALLY A GOOD BROAD.

BINGO.

LIFE'S A CRAP GAME, MILO. I MEAN... I COULD VERY EASILY HAVE BEEN BORN A...A... GARBAGE CAN. RIGHT?

OR A WORM. OR A DOORKNOB. OR...OR A RIPE BANANA. OR I COULD HAVE BEEN BORN A MOLDY SLICE OF SWISS CHEESE! GROSS!

ONION DIP! WHAT IF I'D BEEN BORN A BOWL OF ONION DIP, MILO? HOW AWFUL!

WHAT IF YOU'D BEEN BORN A BABBLING AIRHEAD, BINKLEY?

OH THAT'D BE AWFUL TOO!

WE'VE BEEN HAD, BINKLEY. THE GOVERNMENT HAS DUPED US INTO THINKING THAT WARFARE AND MILITARY MUSCLE IS A FUNCTION OF PATRIOTISM...

THEY'VE MADE A MILITARY STATE THE ACCEPTED NORM! KNOW HOW? BY ASSIMILATING THE WORDS AND SYMBOLS OF WAR RIGHT INTO OUR DAILY CULTURE! THOSE SNEAKS!

≥ SIGH ≤

HAVE SOME BAZOOKA BUBBLE GUM.

THANKS.

MISS HARLOW. I FEEL I MUST PROTEST. COACH BLOOM INSISTS THAT I PARTICIPATE IN SOMETHING CALLED "SUDDEN DEATH."

NOW FRANKLY, I'M NOT SURE WHAT "SUDDEN DEATH" IS, BUT I'M REASONABLY CONFIDENT THAT IT'S ASSOCIATED WITH "CERTAIN DEATH." I QUIT.

PRIVATE BINKLEY! YOU'RE A.W.O.L.! I'LL HAVE YOUR HEAD!

WELL! I SEEM TO HAVE REACHED AN IMPASSE.

MEN, TAKE BINKLEY'S HEAD.

AND IN 1509, THE BRITISH CROWN WENT TO HENRY THE EIGHTH WHICH—

BORING! BORING! BORING!

MAN, LET'S GET WITH IT! WE WANT THE LATEST ON CHARLES AND DIANA. WHADDYA SUPPOSE THE TWO LOVEBIRDS ARE DOIN' RIGHT NOW?

WELL, MILO, I'D LIKE TO THINK THEY'RE ACTING LIKE ANY OTHER TYPICAL NEWLYWEDS.

YOU'D LIKE WHAT?

A HAREM.

I KNOW, CHARLIE! LET'S GO OUT ON THE LAWN AND PLAY FRISBEE!

ALL RIGHT, MY DOVE.

CALL THE BOMB SQUAD! RELEASE THE DOGS! ARRANGE CROWD CONTROL! ALERT THE MEDIA! SET UP THE SATELLITE FEED!

ALL SET.

FORGET IT!

FORGET IT!

MORE TAXES! SEIZE THE LAND! HAND OVER YOUR FIRST BORN! HEAR ME, PEASANT SWINE, OR FEEL THE STEELY KISS OF ME BLADE!

OFF WITH THE DUKE'S 'EAD! OFF WITH THE COOK'S 'EAD! OFF WITH THE CAT'S 'EAD!

WHAT THE 'ECK!! OFF WITH EVERYBODY'S 'EAD!!

WOOSH!

≈ SIGH ≈ MY CHARLIE, THE TYRANT.

YEAH!

OH CHARLIE! LET'S INVITE ALL OF ME OLD FRIENDS OVER FOR OUR THREE-MONTH ANNIVERSARY COCKTAIL PARTY!

NOW DIANA, DEAR... YOU **KNOW** WE 'AVE TO ASSOCIATE WITH THOSE OF OUR **OWN**.

YEAH? LIKE WHO?

WELL...THERE'S KING IDI "BIG PAPA" OOMAN OF EASTERN UGUMBIA.

KING OOMAN?

YEAH.

DOESN'T HE EAT PEOPLE?

WELL NOT AT A BLEEDIN' COCKTAIL PARTY!

HELLO? MR. BINKLEY? THIS IS MILO BLOOM. I'M AFRAID YOUR SON WON'T MAKE IT HOME FOR SUPPER TONIGHT...

WHAT? OH NO... HE'S FINE. WE'RE DOWN AT THE COUNTY GYM... GONNA HAVE A LITTLE WORKOUT...YOU KNOW.

AND MIGHT I ADD, SIR, THAT NONE OF US HERE CAN REMEMBER YOUR SON EVER LOOKING MORE... BREATHTAKING.

IS HE A BOXER? OR A DIP IN HIS UNDERWEAR? ONLY HIS MOTHER KNOWS FOR SURE.

LOOK, MILO... I'M NOT ENTIRELY CERTAIN THAT I'M READY TO GO INTO THE RING.

AND THAT'S WHY I'M GOING TO PUT YOU THROUGH A RIGOROUS TRAINING SESSION...

JUST IMAGINE THIS BAG AS A HUGE MONGOLIAN CANNIBAL COMIN' AT YA... *HERE HE COMES!! QUICK! PUNCH 'IM! HERE HE COMES!!*

BOP!

TO THE RING!

STILL COMIN', MILO.

OKAY...THERE'S THE BELL. NOW GO GET HIM, KID! POUND HIM! HE'S NOTHIN'!

YEAH... RIGHT... NO PROBLEM, YEAH...

HOWDY!

YER GONNA DIE! I'M ALPHONZO ALI! I FLOAT LIKE A BUTTERFLY, STING LIKE A BEE!

THE DUST I'LL BITE, SO I'LL EXIT STAGE RIGHT.

ROPE A DOPE! ROPE A DOPE!!

WELL, "MAD DOG," LET'S TALK ABOUT WHAT YOU'D LIKE FOR CHRISTMAS.

DANDY! HOW ABOUT TICKETS FOR THE NEW YORK BALLET PRODUCTION OF EDVARD GRIEG'S "PEER GYNT?"

NEW SHOULDER PADS? GOOD CHOICE, SON! WHAT'S A FUTURE STAR DEFENSIVE TACKLE WITHOUT NEW SHOULDER PADS?!

SNAP!

WELL! 'OL DAD WILL JUST HAVE TO INFORM OL' SANTA ABOUT THAT EQUIPMENT, EH, "MAD DOG?"

Dear S. Claus,
Kindly keep an eye peeled for any ~~erogenous~~ erroneous information regarding ~~I~~ the Christmas requests

BET YER LOOKIN' FORWARD TO THAT NEW FOOTBALL GEAR FOR CHRISTMAS, EH, SON? YESSIR! YOU'LL BE BASHING SKULLS ON THE OL' GRIDIRON IN NO TIME!

IT SOUNDS PERFECTLY DREADFUL.

I JUST HOPE YOU WERE A GOOD BOY THIS YEAR. SANTA DOESN'T GIVE NEW FOOTBALL GEAR TO BAD LITTLE BOYS YA KNOW, BINKLEY.

Dear S. Claus,
I, M. Binkley, with both malice and premeditation, squash snails. With ecstasy.

HEY, BOBBI! TAKE ME BACK, BABY! I'M IMPROVED... MORE SENSITIVE! LISTEN.

HARLOW

YOU'RE MY WORLD... MY EVERYTHING... YOU'RE THE MEANING TO AN OTHERWISE SHALLOW LIFE. LOVE ME AGAIN AND I SHALL CHERISH YOU LIKE AN... AN... UH...

HARLOW

AUTUMN BLOSSOM.

AUTUMN BLOSSOM. YEAH.

TUESDAY'S "GENERAL HOSPITAL."

SO WHAT?

RLOW

HARSH REALITIES, BINKLEY... PEOPLE CAN'T TAKE 'EM. SOME FOLKS STILL DENY THAT THOMAS JEFFERSON OWNED SLAVES. CAN YOU BELIEVE THAT?

WELL, I...

AND CAN YOU JUST IMAGINE THEIR SHOCK IF THEY HEARD THAT JOHN WAYNE ACTUALLY ADMITTED TO SMOKING MARIJUANA ONCE. HE DID, YA KNOW. HEH HEH...

ZING!

WHEN LIFE KICKS YOU IN THE TUSH, BEST JUST TO STOP AND SOAK IT.

HEY...YOU FRATERNITY DUDES INTERESTED IN COMING TO A MASSIVE NUCLEAR WEAPONS PROTEST RALLY?

ANY CHICKS THERE?

WELL, I... SAY, YOU GUYS GO TO THE SAME TAILOR OR SOMETHING?

OF COURSE.

RIGHT. SO ANYWAY...CAN YOU GUYS MAKE IT TO THE RALLY?

ONLY IF YOU CLEAR IT WITH BOB, OUR CHAPTER PRESIDENT.

GREAT! SO WHICH ONE IS BOB?

WHO CAN TELL?

BEFORE WE START, MR. BINKLEY HERE HAS AN ALTERNATE PROPOSAL FOR SOME GRASS-ROOTS ACTION AGAINST NUCLEAR WAR. LET'S GIVE IT A GOOD LISTEN.

TONIGHT: NUKE ARMS FREEZE VOTE

OKAY. A GROUP OF US COULD SNEAK INTO THE PENTAGON ONE MORNING AND FLUSH ALL 760 TOILETS AT THE SAME TIME, EFFECTIVELY BURSTING THE PIPES AND MAKING THE ENTIRE AMERICAN MILITARY COMPLEX **HIGGLEDY-PIGGLEDY.**

TONIGHT: NUKE FREEZE FREEZE VOTE

THANK YOU. THAT BOGGLED THE MIND.

YEAH!

THANK YOU AND GOOD NIGHT.

"HIGGLEDY-PIGGLEDY" MEANS "A REAL MESS."

WELCOME TO "MISTER ROGERS' NEIGHBORHOOD," BOYS AND GIRLS! WILL YOU BE MY FRIEND TODAY?

GOOD! NOW TODAY WE HAVE A SPECIAL VISITOR TO MY NEIGHBORHOOD... HIS NAME IS SENATOR KRAVITZ.

SENATOR KRAVITZ IS WHAT WE CALL A "PUBLIC SERVANT." MY, IT'S A BIG WORD, ISN'T IT? CAN **YOU** SAY "PUBLIC SERVANT?"

BOZO.

GOOD!

MAY I HELP YOU?

YES. I'D LIKE A HERRING BURGER WITH LOADS OF MAYO.

PUSH — Burger KING

HERRING? AS IN **FISH**?

YES. PENGUINS ARE BIG ON FRESH RAW HERRING!

PUSH — Burger KING

LOOK... THIS IS WEIRD.

SIR...YOUR SIGN SAID I CAN HAVE IT MY WAY, AND MY WAY IS A HERRING ON A BUN WITH LOTS OF MAYONAISE!

PUSH — Burger

HERRING WHOPPER, HEAVY MAYO

HOLD THE HEAD.

PUSH — Burger KING

49

50

GREETINGS AND SALUTATIONS, SIR. PRAY TELL, WHAT IS THE PURPOSE OF YOUR MOBILE ALUMINUM GIZMO, HERE?

CUTTER JOHN

WELL IT SEEMS I'VE GOT A COUPLE OF USELESS LIMBS.

HELLO!.. DID YOU SAY "USELESS LIMBS?"

FLAP! FLAP! FLAP! FLAP! FLAP! FLAP!

BIRDS OF A FEATHER!

OKAY, EVERYBODY... STAY TOGETHER... KEEP THE KIDS QUIET BACK THERE.

GREAT SCOTT... IT'S A COCKROACH MOB.

THE MASSES HAVE BEEN IGNORED FAR TOO LONG! LONG LIVE THE REVOLUTION!

DEATH TO THE GREAT HATED SATANISTIC HOMEOWNER TYRANT.!!

SUPPOSE THAT'S ME?

IMPERIALIST PIG. GIVE US SOME WHEATIES.

UH-OH. WHAT NOW?

POINK!

CUTTER JOHN

LONG LIVE THE GLORIOUS COCKROACH REBELLION AGAINST THE GREAT SUBURBAN BOURGEOIS OPPRESSOR SWINE-PIG.!!

SLAM!

I HATE REVOLUTIONARY JARGON.

MEDIC!

CUTTER HONEY? I KNOW YOU TWO HAVE NEVER MET, BUT MY MOTHER IS OVER HERE AND WANTS TO COOK DINNER FOR US.

SPECIAL OCCASION? YEAH... I'LL TELL YOU WHAT THE SPECIAL OCCASION IS...

SHE WANTS TO SCOPE YOU OUT TOP TO BOTTOM.

BONK!

ER...SHE JUST WANTS TO DUMP OLD LEFTOVERS.

BINKLEY.

I DON'T WANNA HEAR IT, MILO.

DID ADAM AND EVE HAVE NAVELS?

WELL, YOU CAN JUST ROCK ME TO SLEEP, TONIGHT!

YEP. THAT'S A STUMPER.

HELLO? IS THE CALLER THERE?

YES... I'M HERE, MR. DONAHUE.

YOUR COMMENT?

PENGUIN LUST IS NOT "IMMORAL AND WICKED." AND ANYBODY WHO THINKS SO IS JUST AN OLD PRUDE...

IT'S BEAUTIFUL! AND NATURAL! AND I FOR ONE FULLY SUPPORT PENGUIN LUST!

GREAT. BUT TODAY'S TOPIC IS "NUN BEATING."

GOOD LORD, MAN... I CAN'T SUPPORT THAT.

THIS HAD NEVER HAPPENED TO ME BEFORE, BOBBI...YESTERDAY I OVERHEARD SOME JERK INSULTING YOU... AND SUDDENLY, DO YOU KNOW WHAT I WANTED TO DO?

WHAT?

I WANTED TO STAND UP AND BELT HIM ONE! AND OF COURSE I COULDN'T! I COULDN'T!

≋ SMACK! ≋

THATS FOR NOT BEING A DUMB MACHO VIOLENT BRUTE.

I RAN OVER HIS TOES. TWICE.

STEVE DALLAS IS BUGGING ME AGAIN. HE'S VERY JEALOUS, YA KNOW...

AND GET THIS...HE'S CONVINCED THAT I'LL FALL IN LOVE WITH HIM IF HE STARTS ACTING MORE LIKE YOU.

LIKE ME? HOW'S THAT?

YOU DON'T WANT TO KNOW.

OKAY... KEEP YOUR HEAD, STEVE BOY...

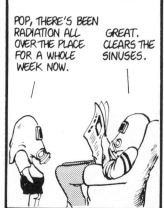

"THE SPLIT-ATOM BLUES"
GIMME TWINKIES, GIMME WINE,
GIMME JEANS BY CALVIN KLEIN...

MILO'S MEADOW

BUT IF YOU SPLIT THOSE ATOMS FINE, MAMA KEEP 'EM OFF THOSE GENES OF MINE!

YEAH!

GIMME ZITS, TAKE MY DOUGH, GIMME ARSENIC IN MY JELLY ROLL...

CALL THE DEVIL AND SELL MY SOUL, BUT MAMA KEEP DEM ATOMS WHOLE!!

YOW!   BEAUTY!

HAD ENOUGH SUN?

I THINK SO.

MILO'S MEADOW

READY TO GO?

YEAH. CAN WE GIVE A FEW FRIENDS A LIFT?

SURE.

CRANK THIS SUCKER UP!

SNIFF!

SNIFF! SNIFF!

LIP-MASHING IS AN ODDITY IN THE WILD KINGDOM.

HEY, BURT. COME HERE AND SEE THIS.

I'M FED UP! THAT'S RIGHT! I'M FED UP WITH ALL OF 'EM!

ME TOO! WHO ARE THEY?

LEFT WINGERS!!

"..ALWAYS SCURRYIN' AROUND YELLIN' "RIGHTS FOR THIS!" AND "RIGHTS FOR THAT!""

FLAP! FLAP! FLAP!

I HATE 'EM!

WELL MAYBE THEY DON'T CARE FOR YOU EITHER.

55

HEY.

YES, SIR?

WAS THAT YOU DOING THAT?

DOING WHAT?

SCREAMING DURING THE PREVIEW OF "SUPERMAN III."

SCREAMING WHAT?

"TAKE IT OFF, LOIS."

HE DID IT.

79¢ FOR A BOX OF BANANA WALRUS WAFERS? THAT'S RIDICULOUS!

LOOK... I ONLY WORK HERE.

WHY ARE CANDY PRICES SO HIGH AT THE MOVIES? 79¢ FOR BANANA WALRUS WAFERS?! THAT'S A SCANDAL!

WELL, SIR... I ADMIT IT'S...UH...

THERE'S NO SUCH THING AS WALRUS WAFERS!

WELL, THERE SHOULD BE.

GOOD EVENING. FRANK REYNOLDS HERE FOR ABC NEWS. TONIGHT'S TOP STORIES: THE U.S. ECONOMY RECOVERS... BANKS LEND MONEY FOR FREE.

OVERSEAS... THE SOVIETS ADMIT THAT COMMUNISM IS A TOTAL REPRESSIVE FAILURE. FREE ELECTIONS CALLED FOR NEXT TUESDAY.

AND JUST IN... COLUMNISTS GEORGE WILL AND BILL BUCKLEY CREATE A LEGAL DEFENSE FUND FOR GAY WELFARE CHEATS.

REALLY?

HA HA... NO.

I WASN'T GOING TO BUY THAT LAST ONE.

DAD! WAKE UP! QUICK! DAD!

WHAT IS IT SON?

DAD! WILL BURT REYNOLDS EVER FIND "MISS RIGHT?" OR IS HE JUST TOO WILD AND FAST FOR ANY REAL STABILITY IN HIS LIFE?!

WELL? WHADDYA THINK?

YOU'VE GOT TO BE KIDDING.

MY FEELINGS EXACTLY... HE'LL SETTLE DOWN SOMEDAY.

"GEORGE PHBLAT'S NEW FILM, 'BENJI SAVES THE UNIVERSE,' HAS BROUGHT THE WORD 'BAD' TO NEW LEVELS OF BADNESS."

TAP TAP TAP

Film CRITIC

"BAD ACTING. BAD EFFECTS. BAD EVERYTHING. THIS BAD FILM JUST OOZED ROTTENNESS FROM EVERY BAD SCENE...SIMPLY BAD BEYOND ALL INFINITE DIMENSIONS OF POSSIBLE BADNESS."

TAP TAP

TAP TAP TAP

"WELL MAYBE NOT THAT BAD, BUT LORD, IT WASN'T GOOD."

Film CRITIC

GREETINGS! I'M HERE FOR MY BIANNUAL HAIRCUT!

WELL! JUST A LIGHT TRIM TODAY I THINK. WATCH THE BACK... I FAVOR A LITTLE FULLNESS AROUND THE FANNY...

...TRIM THE LASHES A TAD...CLIP THE NAILS... SHAMPOO MY TUMMY... THIN THE FLIPPERS AND SHAVE THE FEET.

AND THE NOSE HAIR?

OH, JUST A LAYER CUT FOR THAT NATURAL, READY-FOR-ACTION DISCO LOOK.

WHHIRR...

THERE. HOW DO YOU LIKE IT?

OH MY. WELL. IT CERTAINLY IS A CHANGE, ISN'T IT?

LOOK...YOU WANT A HAIRSTYLE TO MATCH YOUR SINGLE, ON-THE-GO LIFESTYLE.

DO I?

YEAH. BABY, THIS IS YOU.

BUT WILL I GET THE CHICKS? I MEAN, IN TRUCKLOADS?

HELLO? BLOOM BEACON?

HELLO, MRS. BILLSBY. HOW'S THE ARTHRITIS?

CITY DESK

FINE, DEAR, BUT YOU FOLKS PRINTED THAT I DIED.

IMPOSSIBLE. WE DON'T MAKE MISTAKES ON THE OBITUARY PAGE, MRS. BILLSBY.

BUT I'M LOOKING AT IT RIGHT HERE.

.OKAY...FIND SOME GOOD LIGHT AND READ IT TO ME SLOWLY.

CITY DESK

"BILLSBY SLASHES FOUR, DIES IN COCAINE BRAWL"

THAT'S THE FRONT PAGE, MRS. BILLSBY.

CITY DESK

62

SIR! WE'RE READY TO BOARD SHIP AND EXPLORE NEW WORLDS!

SORRY, CREW. NO MISSION TODAY.

DID YOU HEAR THAT, MR. SULU? SOMETHING MUST BE AMISS.

GRAB YER TRI-CORDER, SPOCK. LET'S TAKE A LOOK.

SNIFF SNIFF

WELL?

THE CAPTAIN... HAS A TOMATO.

CLEAR THE BRIDGE PLEASE.

PSSST! BINKLEY!... OVER HERE!...

ON BEHALF OF MYSELF AND THE REST OF YOUR SUBCONSCIOUS ANXIETIES, WE THOUGHT YOU SHOULD BE GIVEN ADVANCE NOTICE REGARDING OUR PLAN TO JUMP OUT AND GRAB YOU THIS EVENING.

THANK YOU.

CERTAINLY.

A CLOSET FULL OF COURTEOUS ANXIETIES IS OF DUBIOUS COMFORT.

LOOK...JUST EXACTLY WHO ARE ALL OF YOU HIDING IN THERE?

YOUR ANXIETIES!... FIGMENTS OF YOUR FANCY, THAT'S WHO!...

...MONSTERS AND MINOTAURS... CREATURES AND CREEPIES... BUGS AND BEARS AND BATS AND OTHER PIECES OF YOUR PERSONAL WHIMSY.

WHY, THERE ARE EVEN A FEW CELEBRITIES! MAYBE WE COULD ARRANGE FOR PHYLLIS SCHLAFLY TO JUMP OUT AND GRAB YOU SOMETIME.

HOW ABOUT VICTORIA PRINCIPAL?

WE'RE NIGHTMARES. PIPE DREAMS ARE UNDER THE BED.

I HEAR YOU IN THAT CLOSET! WHICH OF MY 20TH CENTURY ANXIETIES ARE YOU THIS TIME?! DARTH VADER? NUKE BOMBS? RING AROUND THE COLLAR?!

WELL I'M GOING TO FACE MY FEARS! DID YOU HEAR ME?! I'M COMING IN! DID YOU HEAR ME?!

AAIGHH!

A THOUSAND PARDONS. I THOUGHT THIS WAS THE JOHN.

ALL ENGINES STOP, MR. SULU.

AN INTRUDER HAS DOCKED HIS CORVETTE IN THE HANDICAPPED DOCKING SPACE!

LET'S TORPEDO THIS KLINGON-BRAIN INTO SPACE DUST.!

YEAH! EAT ANTI-MATTER, YOU SPACE DUD.! TELL 'IM MR. SPOCK!

A POX ON YOUR FIRST BORN, YOU UGLY WART ON A SALAMANDER'S TONGUE!

...OR WAS THAT OUT OF CHARACTER?

NO! NO! THAT WAS JUST ★@#? SPIFFY.!

MAYBE I SHOUDN'T HAVE REQUESTED THIS TRANSFER TO THE BEACON'S NEW "PERSONALS" SECTION...

PLACE ADS HERE

CLASSIFIED PERSONALS

ADVERTISING FOR A MATE IN THE CLASSIFIEDS... PRETTY WEIRD STUFF IF YOU ASK ME.

DEADLINE: 4:30 PM

The Bloom Beacon

JUST IMAGINE WHAT KIND OF NUT THIS SORT OF THING ATTRACTS...

CLASSIFIED PERSONALS

JUST IMAGINE.

"FABULOUSLY HANDSOME SINGLE MALE, 28, SEEKS TOMATO, 18-22, FOR MANHANDLING AND LIGHT HOUSECLEANING."

CLASSIFIED PERSONALS

IS THIS WHERE I CAN PLACE AN AD IN THE "PERSONALS?"

SURELY. HOW WOULD YOU LIKE IT TO READ?

CLASSIFIED PERSONALS

"SINGLE, RED-HEADED FEMALE, 23, SENSUAL, INTELLIGENT, DELICIOUS; SEEKS SHORT, FLIGHTLESS, AQUATIC BIRD ON WHICH TO LAVISH KISSES AND AFFECTION."

CLASSIFIED PERSONALS

THANKS. HERE'S MY NUMBER IF I GET LUCKY.

CLASSIFIED PERSONALS

AS GOD IS MY WITNESS, I HAVEN'T THE FAINTEST IDEA WHAT I SHOULD DO.

CLASSIFIED PERSONALS

HAPPY POST VALENTINE'S DAY, BABY. HERE... I GOT YA SOMETHING.

I HOPE YOU LIKE IT.

A BOX OF OBSCENELY SHAPED CHOCOLATES.

YEP. A CLASSY GIFT FOR A CLASSY BROAD...BE MINE FOREVER, TOOTS. =SMACK!=

A QUESTION...

YEAH, BABY?

WHO ARE YOU?

WE'RE BACK! THIS IS ROCKIN' CHARMIN' HARMON HERE AT **KRNA**... THE STATION THAT ROCKS BLOOM COUNTY!

SAY, ROCKERS... IF A "MIKE BINKLEY" IS OUT THERE, GIVE ME A RING, PAL.. SOMEBODY FOUND YOUR SCHOOLBAG AND TURNED IT IN TO OL' CHARMIN' HARMON...

UH-OH... HEY BINKLEY BABE! LOOKS LIKE YA GOT AN OVERDUE LIBRARY BOOK HERE... LESSEE...

"BED-WETTING: BEAT IT THROUGH SELF-HYPNOSIS."

OKAY... NOW BACK TO THE MUSIC...

NOW FOR AN UPDATE... THE IRISH STILL HATE THE ENGLISH.. THE ARABS STILL HATE THE JEWS.. THE JEWS STILL HATE THE PALESTINIANS.. THE IRANIANS S[T]... THE IRAQI... HATE CH[R]... [MU]SLEMS.

≋ CLICK ≋

MASS DANDELION BREAK.

Now THEN, BEING FOR THE MOMENT WITHOUT A PRESIDENTIAL CANDIDATE, THE NOMINATING COMMITTEE SET TO WORK NAMING THE UNLUCKY INDIVIDUAL TO THE THANKLESS ROLE OF **VICE-PRESIDENTIAL** CANDIDATE.

NATIONAL RADICAL MEADOW PARTY

CAUCUS IN SESSION

QUICKLY WERE THE DEBATES DEBATED, THE DISCUSSIONS DISCUSSED AND THE VOTES VOTED...

ALL OF WHICH RESULTED IN A REMARKABLY UNANIMOUS DECISION. THE MEADOW PARTY'S VICE-PRESIDENTIAL CANDIDATE WAS TO BE...

OPUS. OPUS. OPUS.

...WHO, OF COURSE, HAD RECENTLY BEEN DISPATCHED TO THE FOODMART FOR SOME "CHEETOS" TO INSURE A SMOOTH NOMINATION.

I DON'T LIKE THE LOOKS OF THIS.

AND SO THE MEADOW PARTY'S NOMINEE FOR THE VICE-PRESIDENCY RETIRES TO PONDER THIS NEW AND WHOLLY UNSOLICITED SITUATION...

≋ SIGH ≋

JUST HOW **DO** THEY EXPECT A FELLOW TO PROPERLY PREPARE FOR THOSE SPECIFIC DUTIES AND RESPONSIBILITIES OF AN AMERICAN VICE-PRESIDENT?

OPUS WAS, OF COURSE, A NATURAL FOR THE JOB.

ZZZ ≋ SNORT ≋

THE...THE WHOLE THING STARTED WHEN I BUMPED INTO JACKIE AT THE CARROT JUICE COUNTER DURING A "SAVE THE WHALES" BENEFIT PICNIC. SHE SAID I OUGHT TO WRITE THAT BOOK WE'D DISCUSSED BACK AT BERKELEY IN '68.

SO I SAID, "WHAT THE HECK", AND BORROWED AN OLD SMITH-CORONA FROM ABBIE AT THE WORLD HUNGER COUNCIL, SCRAPED A FEW BUCKS TOGETHER AND PUBLISHED THAT LITTLE BABY MYSELF.

I TITLED IT "THE AMERICAN RICH: FORGOTTEN FINANCIAL FASCISTS." IT WENT THROUGH 22 PRINTINGS. I NETTED OVER A QUARTER MILLION.

SLURP!

TODAY MY ACCOUNTANT RAN UP AND GAVE ME A HUG AND SAID, "CONGRATULATIONS, LARRY... YOU SAVED $91,000 LAST YEAR WITH REAGAN'S TAX CUT."

WHAT'S A LIBERAL TO DO?!

HIT ME AGAIN AND PUT IT ON THAT GUY'S TAB.

WHERE'S MILO TODAY?

AT HOME WATCHING SOMETHING NEW ON CABLE CALLED "MTV".. ROCK VIDEOS OR SOMETHING...

HELLO. I'M FROM THE BUREAU OF NOSY STATISTICS. WOULD YOU ANSWER SOME QUESTIONS?

CERTAINLY, MADAM.

WHAT IS YOUR WEIGHT? HEIGHT? PANTS SIZE? AND SEXUAL PREFERENCE?

36 POUNDS. 2'11". I DON'T WEAR ANY PANTS. SVELTE, BUOYANT WATERFOWL.

THANK YOU.

MY PLEASURE.

THEY'RE EITHER GOING TO ARREST ME OR FIRE HER.

ZZ...

YAWN

CLICK ...ARE THE THREE THINGS ANNOUNCED JUST TODAY WHICH HAVE BEEN FOUND TO CAUSE MASSIVE, FATAL NOSE WARTS IN PENGUINS. FOR CBS NEWS...GOODNIGHT.

WHAT?! NO! WAIT! GO BACK! COME AGAIN?!

STAY TUNED FOR "HAPPY DAYS."

OH MY LORD...

SHOULDN'T HAVE BEEN NAPPING.

SOME TIME AGO... IN A BED FAR, FAR AWAY...

...LAY A YOUNG JEDI KNIGHT... WHO, AFTER A DINNER OF SPICY, CREAMED ARTICHOKES, WAS HAVING A ...SHALL WE SAY, LESS THAN PEACEFUL SLEEP...

REBEL LEADER! THIS IS LUKE BINKLEYWALKER! I'VE GOT PRINCESS PISTACHIO...BUT THERE'S A GIANT BURGER KING "DARTH VADER" DEATH GLASS ON MY BUTT!!

UH...HELLO. ARE YOU AN ANXIETY OF MINE?

AN ANXIETY **TO BE**. I'M BETSY MARPLE... THE FIRST GIRL YOU'LL EVER KISS.

IT'LL BE DURING A JUNIOR HIGH SCHOOL PARTY IN 1988... ABOUT 60 PEOPLE WILL BE WATCHING WHEN YOU'LL BEND OVER TO KISS ME AND MISS MY MOUTH BY A FULL THREE INCHES, NEARLY SEVERING MY RIGHT NOSTRIL WITH YOUR BRACES WHILE YOU KNOCK A BOWL OF BEAN DIP DOWN THE FRONT OF MY DRESS...

...ALL OF WHICH WILL LEAVE ME AN EMOTIONAL WRECK FOR THE REST OF MY TRAUMATIZED ADOLESCENT LIFE. YOU'RE NOT FEELING GUILTY ABOUT THIS, ARE YOU?

OH, NO.

EVENTUALLY, OF COURSE, I ENDED UP IN A LESBIAN TERRORIST GROUP...

ANTS!! ANTS IN THE BATHROOM! BIG, LARGE, HAIRY ANTS! WITH FANGS! ALL OVER!

LOTS OF 'EM! AT LEAST...

WELL... AT LEAST ONE. ON THE TOILET SEAT.

ONE **DEAD** ANT ACTUALLY.

TO EACH HIS HANG-UP.

WAIT...BEFORE YOU BRING OUT ANY MORE OF MY ANXIETIES TONIGHT... JUST...JUST PROMISE ME ONE THING...

CERTAINLY!

WHATEVER YOU DO, DON'T... PLEASE...**DON'T** SEND OUT **NASTASSJA KINSKI** TO GIVE ME A SWEDISH MASSAGE!

YEAH?

YEAH. OH, ANYTHING BUT THAT! AWFUL! AWFUL! AWFUL!

OKAY BOYS... SEND OUT KINSKI!!!

...WITH A BIG SLICE OF CHEESECAKE.

...WITH A BIG SLI-- ...HOLD IT.

THIS IS TOMORROW'S UNSUBSTANTIATED "HOT N' JUICY" GOSSIP?

IT IS.

"OUR INSIDERS WHISPER THAT BARBARA WALTERS IS HEALING A NEW FACE IN CAPE COD WITH LOVE SLAVE CHARLES KURALT."

MY. THIS **DOES** SEEM HOT N' JUICY.

YEP.

THE EAR

I'LL JUST RUN IT BY OUR HOT N' JUICY LAWYERS.

NOW LET'S NOT GET IRRATIONAL.

THE EAR

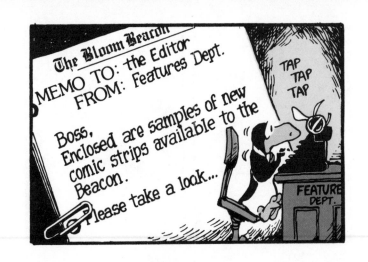

SNAKE. THERE'S A SNAKE IN THE WATER.

WHERE?

RIGHT BELOW. I'M NOT GOING IN.

GROSS. IT'S HUGE.

WHO SAID SNAKE?

NOW WHAT?

I CALL FOR UNRESTRAINED PANIC.

YA KNOW, VOLTAIRE ONCE SAID THAT THERE'S A CERTAIN INEVITABLE FUTILITY IN INDECISION...

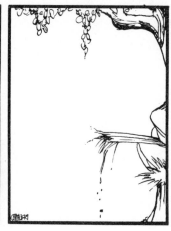

THUS...WITH THE DISCOVERY OF LEGLESS REPTILES IN THE LOCAL SWIMMING HOLE, QUICK ACTION WAS CLEARLY IN ORDER... ACTION WHICH HISTORY BOOKS WOULD EVENTUALLY CALL "THE GREAT BLOOM COUNTY SNAKE MASSACRE."

IT WOULD BE A DAY TO REMEMBER...

...BOLDLY THE MIGHTY SNAKE SLAUGHTERERS SET FORTH...

BOLDLY THE MIGHTY SNAKE SLAUGHTERERS SET FORTH...

DON'T RUSH US.

NOW, ALTHOUGH THE GREAT BLOOM COUNTY SNAKE MASSACRE WAS NOT WELL DOCUMENTED, CERTAIN CRUCIAL SKIRMISHES HAVE INDEED BECOME QUITE FAMOUS...

SEE ANYTHING?

AAIGH!

WHAM!! WHAM! WHAM WHAM WHAM

...HOWEVER, THE "BATTLE OF SHADY CREEK," ALTHOUGH DECISIVE, WAS QUICKLY AND WISELY FORGOTTEN.

THE GREAT SNAKE MASSACRE WAS TO CONTINUE...THE VIOLENCE AND CARNAGE GETTING TO BE, AT TIMES, JUST SIMPLY AWFUL.

SCORE THUS FAR ...
SNAKES : 1
INSUFFICIENTLY BUOYANT SNAKE SLAUGHTERER : 0

NOW, IF THERE ARE THOSE WHO DOUBT THE WORLDLY SIGNIFICANCE OF THE GREAT SNAKE MASSACRE, THERE ARE ALSO THOSE WHO KNOW THAT LIFE'S GREATEST JOYS ARE ITS MINOR TRIUMPHS. IT IS TO THIS LATTER GROUP THAT WE DEDICATE THAT DAY IN WHICH THE ALL-VOLUNTEER GROUP OF FEARLESS SNAKE SLAUGHTERERS SUCCEEDED IN BEATING SENSELESS A BATTERY CABLE FROM A '73 PINTO.

IT'S LATE AT THE BLOOM BEACON... AND MILO HAS BEEN EDITING THE COMICS PAGE..

ZZZ...
COMICS...COMICS... EVERYWHERE...COMICS...

I WONDER... I WONDER WHAT IT'S LIKE TO WORK AS A...A...

...A NATIONALLY SYNDICATED CARTOONIST...

ZZOO

I SAID FUNNIER!! PLEASE! NOT THE WHIP!

Acme PRESS SYNDICAT

MILO DREAMS OF BEING A SYNDICATED CARTOONIST...

I DON'T GET THIS ONE. YOU'LL HAVE TO BE PUNISHED.

Acme PRESS SYNDICATE

WAIT! LET ME EXPLAIN, BOSS... UH...I MEAN IT'S SORT OF ABSTRACT... SEE, THIS DOG GOES OVER THERE... AND THEN THIS CAT COMES UP AND...WELL...SEE?

IT'S MOSTLY VISUAL. DO YOU GET IT NOW? WELL? BOSS?

GET THE BOX OF LEECHES, MISS HORNWINKLE.

LEMME WORK ON IT...

THAT'S IT, BLOOM... YOU MISSPELLED THE WORD "XANTHELASMOIDEA" IN TODAY'S STRIP. YOU THINK ALL WE EDITORS HAVE TO DO IS CORRECT YOUR DUMB MISTAKES?

WHERE ARE YOU TAKING ME?!

TO THE BOTTOMLESS PIT OF ARTISTIC MISSPELLERS! AAIGH!

POOF!

Features

MY GOODNESS, FOLKS...HAVE YOU EVER THOUGHT ABOUT THE AWESOME DEBT WE ALL OWE TO CARTOONIS—

OH CUT THAT OUT.

Features

I'D NEVER CRY IF I DID FIND A BLUE WHALE IN MY SOUP...

NOR WOULD I MIND A PORCUPINE INSIDE A CHICKEN COOP.

YES LIFE IS FINE WHEN THINGS COMBINE, LIKE HAM IN BEEF CHOW MEIN...

BUT LORD, THIS TIME I THINK I MIND, THEY'VE PUT ACID IN MY RAIN.

≡BEEP!≡ YOU HAVE REACHED THE MAIN COMPUTER AT THE NATIONAL STRATEGIC DEFENSE CENTER IN COLORADO. FURTHER ACCESS PROHIBITED WITHOUT SPECIAL HIGH-LEVEL CODE SEQUENCE.

BLIP BEEP! CLICK BLIP BEEP! CLICK BEEP

CODE SEQUENCE APPROVED. GREETINGS, MR. PRESIDENT.

PIECE O' CAKE.

SHALL WE DUST MOSCOW?

≡BEEP≡ YOU HAVE REACHED BELL TELEPHONE'S CUSTOMER-ACCOUNT FILE. ENTRY IS STRICTLY PROHIBITED WITHOUT INCREDIBLY COMPLEX SECURITY-ACCESS CODE.

AVAST, YE SCURVY CORPORATE SWABS!! PREPARE TO BE BOARDED!

TAP TAP CLICK BEEP CLICK CLICK BEEP CLICK

≡BEEP≡ ENTRY APPROVED.

ON TO PILLAGE!

THAT'S IT. I'VE BROKEN INTO THE NEW YORK TIMES STORY FILE.

SUPERB, OLIVER.

HAVE THEY COMPOSED TOMORROW'S FRONT-PAGE HEADLINE YET?

UH...YES. RIGHT HERE: "REAGAN CALLS WOMEN 'AMERICA'S MOST VALUABLE RESOURCE.'"

NO NO NO. TOO WORDY. LET'S JUST TIGHTEN THAT BABY UP A BIT...

CLICK... CLICK...

TODAY, THE NEW YORK TIMES INSISTED THAT YESTERDAY'S HEADLINE QUOTING PRESIDENT REAGAN AS SAYING THAT WOMEN WERE "LITTLE DUMPLINS" WAS A RESULT OF COMPUTER PIRACY.

"SOMEBODY OUT THERE GAINED ACCESS TO OUR STORY FILE AND MADE THE CHANGES," SAID PERPLEXED COPY EDITOR JILL SMITH.

NEVERTHELESS, THIS MORNING 200,000 FEMINISTS PELTED THE WHITE HOUSE WITH OVER A MILLION DUMPLINGS, PROMPTING THE MOBILIZATION OF THE 101ST AIRBORNE. TONIGHT, THE NATION'S CAPITAL REMAINS IN TOTAL CHAOS.

THE WONDER OF IT ALL!

"WELL *I'D* BE THE PRESIDENT'S LITTLE DUMPLIN *ANYDAY*," SAID PHYLLIS SCHLAFLY EARLIER.

OLIVER, I'VE JUST RECEIVED A REFUND CHECK FROM THE I.R.S. COMPUTER. IT'S FOR $1.8 MILLION.

OH, THAT'S GREAT, POP. BUY YOURSELF A NEW CAR.

OLIVER

NOW LOOK HERE, MISTER "HACKER..."

LISTEN, DAD... IF YOU DON'T KEEP IT, IT'LL JUST GO TO BUILD NUCLEAR BOMBS.

NOW SON... THAT'S A...UH, THAT'S...WELL...ER...

LOOK... I DON'T NEED THESE MORAL DILEMMAS...

BUICKS OR BOMBS, POP. CINCH.

OLIVER

TIC TIC TIC TIC

ATTENTION, INTRUDER: THIS IS THE CENTRAL I.R.S. COMPUTER OFFICE. YOU ARE CONDUCTING AN ILLEGAL INTRUSION INTO I.R.S. FILES. IDENTIFY YOURSELF.

REPEAT: IDENTIFY IMMEDIATELY.

WAIT... HERE WE GO... "STE... "STEVE DALLAS.."

HEY, GET THIS DOWN!

US GOVT.

WHO'S KNOCKIN' ON MY FRONT DOOR AT 5:00 IN THE ★☺#?! MORNING ?!

THE F.B.I., MR. DALLAS. YOU'RE UNDER SUSPICION OF DATA TRESPASSING AND COMPUTER PIRACY. OPEN UP.

TOTAL GIBBERISH. MUST BE DRUNK... PROBABLY A BUNCH OF MY OLD FRAT BROTHERS... AWRIGHT, GUYS...

KNOCK! KNOCK!

YAAAA!

PHOOSH!

FIRE

THAT OUGHTA SOBER 'EM UP.

KNOCK! KNOCK!

FIRE

ALL RIGHT, MR. DALLAS... YOU'VE BEEN CHARGED WITH BREAKING INTO GOVERNMENT COMPUTER FILES... I'VE BEEN FRAMED, JUDGE. I DIDN'T DO IT. I SWEAR... I DIDN'T DO IT!

MR. DALLAS... I'VE BEEN LISTENING TO YOU ALL DAY AND I'VE REACHED ONE INESCAPABLE CONCLUSION...

...YOU HAVEN'T THE BRAINS TO SUCCESSFULLY PICK YOUR NOSE, MUCH LESS WORK A COMPUTER.

NEXT CASE. WHAM! WELL MAYBE I DID DO IT!!

HEY, THIS LOOKS GOOD... A WAR MOVIE! UH, ACTUALLY I THINK IT'S AN ABC DOCUMENTARY ON LEBANON. I THINK.

OH PHOO. LOOKS LIKE AN OLD "RAT PATROL" EPISODE. NO... NO, IT'S JUST THE 6 O'CLOCK NEWS. I THINK. THOSE LOOK LIKE REAL GRENADE LAUNCHERS.

YEAH! BLAST THAT SUCKER! OO! THIS IS GREAT STUFF!! BLAM! BLAM!

WELL. I MEAN IF IT IS FAKE. WILL SOMEONE PLEASE TELL ME WHETHER I SHOULD BE ENJOYING THIS OR NOT...

OH DAD...THIS IS SHOCKING. THIS IS HORRIBLE. SEZ HERE IN "PEOPLE" THAT THEY GAVE MARIEL HEMINGWAY "BREAST IMPLANTS" FOR HER NEW MOVIE "STAR 80."

WELL, SIR... WHAT I'D LIKE TO KNOW IS JUST WHAT, EXACTLY, DID THOSE DEVILS PLANT IN THAT POOR WOMAN'S CHEST? BEAN SPROUTS? ALFALFA?! TULIPS?!

FER GOODNESS SAKE... I'VE NEVER HEARD OF SUCH A THING. WHY JUST LOOK AT THESE PICTURES OF HER, DAD... DAD? LOOK AT THIS...

NO!! GREAT SCOTT. THEY MUST'VE PLANTED CANTALOUPES.

BINKLEY! OH, BINKLEY! WE HAVE A FULL MENU OF ANXIETIES TONIGHT!! PLEASE CHOOSE THE NIGHTMARE OF YOUR CHOICE FROM THE FOLLOWING:

A: JESSE HELMS EXPLAINING AT LENGTH HOW MARTIN LUTHER KING WAS A COMMUNIST, B: A CONVENTION OF "PM MAGAZINE" HOSTS. C: A HUGE, BINKLEY-EATING PYTHON.

I'LL TAKE THE PYTHON. GREAT! I'LL SEND IT RIGHT OUT!

HECK, I'M NO GLUTTON FOR PUNISHMENT.

THE BILL CAT STORY

THE

Part 1:
The Early,
Innocent Years

It was in the green, gentle hills of Dubuque, Iowa, that a simple country cat named Bill first dreamed of becoming somebody... of becoming a famous cartoon star...

BILLIE...YA AIN'T GONNA FERGIT 'BOUT ME WHEN YA GET FAMOUS, ARE YA, BILLIE?

ACK.

So, leaving behind his hills, his girl and his old life, Bill set out for the place where dreams come true... NEW YORK CITY!

SAY HI TO "MARMADUKE" FER ME, BILLIE BOY!

ACK!

NEW YORK WON'T BITE

...but New York can be a cruel town. After months of humiliating rejections by such industry giants as "The Family Circus" and "Beetle Bailey"... Bill found himself at the back door of the scruffiest, grungiest feature in town...

YEAH...WE COULD USE A CAT. DO YA MOP FLOORS?

BLO COUN

And thus...America opened up their Sunday papers that next week to find the genius of a cat named...BILL.

TOMORROW! TOMORROW! I'LL BITE YA, TOMORROW!...

IT'S ONLY A LITTER BOX AWAY!

Yes...a star had been born. A brilliant, shining new star on the comics horizon... the simple, country cat from Iowa had arrived!

NEXT WEEK:
"THE DARK SIDE OF FAME"

RollingStone

BILL
HE'S HOT.
HE'S HIP.
AND HE'S HAIRY.

THE BILL CAT STORY

THE

Part **2**:
Trouble in
the Fast Lane

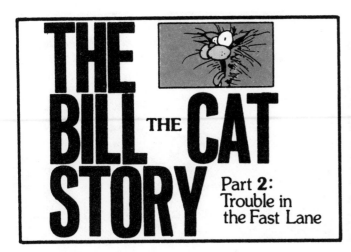

YES, THE SIMPLE, COUNTRY CAT FROM IOWA HAD FOUND WILD SUCCESS ON AMERICA'S COMIC PAGES....AS WELL AS A WAY OF LIFE HE HAD ONLY DARED DREAM OF...

ACK!
VROOM!!

..AND A WAY OF LIFE, WE SHOULD ADD, WHICH WAS TO PROVE INCREASINGLY...DANGEROUSLY SEDUCTIVE...

BILLIE? THIS IS SALLY, BILLIE...WHEN YA COMIN' BACK HOME TO ME, BILLIE?...

HEY BILL! THIS IS HEATHCLIFF! LET'S GET GARFIELD AND GO CRUISIN' FOR BABES!

BILL...LISTEN TO ME, BILL...YOU'RE ACTING IRRESPONSIBLE...YOU'RE FLAUNTING YOUR WEALTH...YOU'RE SNORTIN' DRUGS... YOU'RE VALUES ARE SHOT...BILL! DON'T YOU SEE?..YOU'RE BECOMING A...A...

PROPS
COKE

..., A CELEBRITY!!

AUGH!

THE TRUTH HURT. BUT SO DID THE LONELINESS... WAS *THIS* SUCCESS? WAS <u>THIS</u> COMICS FAME?

NEXT WEEK: "A NEW, BRIEF HOPE"

BRAZIL COCAIN

THE BILL THE CAT STORY

Part 3: The Final Days

Yes, Bill the Cat had come too far, too fast... and had hit bottom...hard. And there, among the pills... the booze...the loose women...his friends pulled him back from the brink...

KEEP WALKING BILL!!

HE'S BEEN FREE-BASING "LITTLE FRISKIES" AGAIN.

So, for a brief, hopeful time, Bill's life and career looked back on track: new merchandising deals.. his face on McDonald's drinking glasses...even a guest appearance on "Fantasy Island."
Yes...Bill had come back.

Move over, Gary Coleman,

People weekly

BILL the CAT

He's off the drugs and high on life.

On September 30th, 1983, Bill drove his Ferrari down Route 66... and into oblivion. The police said he must have been going 140 when he hit the cactus. His body was never found...the circumstances never disclosed. "Death by acne" they said.

VROOM!!

YIKES!

Yes, the light that burns brightest, burns briefest... and his shone oh so bright! We shall not quickly forget Bill ...the cat too fast to live... too gross to die.

OBLIVION AHEAD

THE END

THANK YOU FOR JOINING US, LADIES AND GENTLEMEN... WE HOPE THAT YOU'VE FOUND ALL THIS DONE WITH CLASS AND GOOD TASTE.

FOR A CHANGE.

BILL LIVES

Y...YOU'RE FROM MY ANXIETY CLOSET? YES. WE'RE TWO EXPERT ECONOMISTS. WE'LL BE YOUR NIGHTMARE TONIGHT.

TWO ECONOMISTS?! IN THE SAME ROOM? PLEASE... JUST DON'T DISCUSS THE ECONOMY! THE ECONOMY? OH, IT'S IMPROVING! NO, IT'S NOT.

GENTLE-MEN... THE LEADING ECONOMIC INDI-CATORS SHOW A SUSTAINED RENOBERATION TOWARDS— PHOOEY! THE DEFICIT! WHAT OF THE DEFICIT!

AAIGH! THE KEY, OF COURSE, IS THE DEFICIT. THE DEFICIT, MY FANNY...

I WOULD IMAGINE, BINKLEY, THAT THERE COMES A TIME IN EVERY MAN'S LIFE FOR SOME BRUTAL SELF-RECKONING ...

A TIME TO WEIGH ONESELF ON THE SCALE OF HUMAN WORTH...

...A TIME TO FACE THE GREAT SWIRLING MAELSTROM OF LIFE AND ASK: AM I A ROCK...?

...OR A LEAF?!

SO! I UNDERSTAND YOUR MOTHER'S BEEN WORKING ALL DAY TO TURN YOU INTO "HER OWN LITTLE MICHAEL JACKSON", EH, SON? TRAGICALLY, IT IS TRUE.

WELL, YA LOOK TERRIFIC! BOY, SHE DIDN'T MISS A DETAIL, DID SHE? NOPE! NOT A SINGLE... UH...

SON... WHERE'Z THE REST OF YOUR EYEBROWS? FLOATING IN THE HALL TOILET.

PAD PAD PAD

HELLO! YES OH YES I'D LIKE TO TAKE ADVANTAGE OF YOUR ONCE-IN-A-LIFETIME SPECIAL TV OFFER FOR THE AMAZING RONCO COMBINATION "PLUM PITTER AND YOGURT SQUIRTER" FOR ONLY $39.98!!

IT DICES! IT SLICES! IT SHPLICES! IT PUSHES! IT MOOSHES! IT SQOOSHES! TRULY A DREAM MACHINE! DON'T FORGET THE FREE BONUS "POCKET DIAPER STEAMER!" I'LL TAKE SIX THOUSAND!! THANK YOU! GOOD-BYE!!

AWRIGHT... THAT'S IT. NO MORE LATE-NIGHT TV FOR YOU. YES...YES, THAT'D PROBABLY BE FOR THE BEST...

Panel 1: ALAS...THE SCENE AT "BOB'S BAR AND FLESH MARKET" SIMPLY WASN'T VERY PRETTY...

I AM *RUINED.*

Panel 2: ...DRIED-OUT HULKS OF FRUSTRATED BACHELORHOOD LAY ROTTING ON THE SINGLES BEACH OF LIFE AS THE TIDE OF THE SEXUAL REVOLUTION QUICKLY RECEDES...

SIGH...

Panel 3: ...TRAGIC REFUGEES...ALONE IN THE COLD, CELIBATE WINTER OF THE '80s...

DOESN'T...DOESN'T *ANYBODY* WANT TO SHARE MY PERSONAL SPACE TONIGHT?

Panel 4: YES, AN ERA WAS OVER. AND NONE WERE TO SUFFER MORE THAN THE SEXY AND FORMERLY ACTIVE MEMBERS OF THE OFFICIAL "BLOOM COUNTY *STUD SQUAD*"...

WELL! THIS IS A *FINE* HOW-DO-YOU-DO!
YEAH!
I...I CAN'T TAKE TAKE ANOTHER NIGHT OF "TRIVIAL PURSUIT."

Panel 5: DRESSING FOR THE CONVENTION NEXT WEEK, EH, MR. CANDIDATE? PREPARED TO FACE THE ISSUES?

NATURALLY. I'VE ALWAYS SAID THAT ONE'S POLITICAL POSITIONS SHOULD BE AS NEAT AND TIDY AS THE *KNOT* IN ONE'S *NECKTIE.*

Panel 6: WHAT'S YOUR POSITION ON THE NATIONAL DEBT?
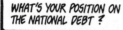

FIBULATE THE INTEREST RATES. RENOOBERATE THE MONEY MARKETS. AND PRINT MORE DOUGH.

Panel 7: AND NICARAGUA?

WELL, THE "CONTRAS"...FUNDED BY THE E.R.A...UH, UNDER THE AUSPICES OF GEMAYAL...ER...THE SANDINISTER...RATHER...STOP THE TERRORIST NETWORK OF GUATAMELON *GORILLAS SMUGGLING EXPLOSIVE PAPAYAS* INTO OHIO. *PERIOD.*

Panel 8: SOUNDS GOOD!

AND LOOKIN' *SHARP!*

Panel 9: HENCE, THE MIGHTY BLOOM COUNTY DELEGATION PROCEEDED TO SPEED WESTWARD TOWARD SAN FRANCISCO. ONWARD THEY WENT!...THROUGH THE SUNBLESSED WARMTH OF THE KANSAS HEART-LAND...

PUTT PUTT PUTT

Panel 10: ...PAST THE AWESOME GRANDEUR OF THE COLORADO ROCKIES...

PUTT PUTT PUTT PUTT

Panel 11: ...THROUGH THE TOWERING MAJESTY OF THE ARIZONA DESERT...

VRROOOM!

Panel 12: ...THROUGH THE SUNBLESSED WARMTH OF THE KANSAS HEART--

SOMEBODY GET OUT THE DAMNED MAP!
PUTT! PUTT! PUTT!

Panel 13: AH! WELCOME TO SAN FRANCISCO! LOVELY TO SEE YOU ALL. PLEASE SIGN IN.

Bob + Ernie's CASTRO St. HOTEL

Panel 14: *FRONT!*

DING! DING!

Panel 15: THIS IS MY PARTNER, ERNIE. HE'LL TAKE YOUR BAGS.
HELLO!

Bob + E, CASTRO HOTI

Panel 16: WHAT SHOULD I TIP HIM?
JUST STOMP ON HIS HEAD. HE LOVES IT.
OH, *STOP* IT!

Bob + CAS H

"HIGH FLIGHT"
BY JOHN GILLESPIE MAGEE, JR.
Oh, I have slipped the surly bonds of earth,
And danced the skies on laughter-silvered wings;
Sunward I've climbed, and joined the tumbling mirth
Of sun-split clouds...and done a hundred things

...You have not dreamed of...wheeled and soared
and swung
High in the sunlit silence. Hov'ring there,

FLAP
FLAP
FLAP

I've chased the shouting wind along, and flung
My eager craft through footless halls of air.

YA! YA! YA! YA! YA!

Up, up, the long, delirious
burning blue
I've topped the windswept
heights with easy grace
Where never lark, or
even eagle flew.

And while with silent, lifting mind I've trod
The high untrespassed sanctity of space...

WHOA...

...put out my hand, and touched
the face of God.

LAST
RITES!

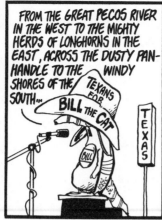

SAY, OPUS...THE BARBARA JORDAN DEAL FELL THROUGH. WE'D LIKE TO KNOW IF YOU'D ACCEPT THE V.P. SPOT AGAIN.

YES! YES! THANK YOU! THANK YOU! OF COURSE! ALLOW ME TO KISS YOUR FEET! I'LL ACCEPT! I'LL ACCEPT! I'LL ACCEPT!!

POINK POINK

MAYBE.

WELL, IT'S DONE, MILO. BILL THE CAT IS OUR OFFICIAL PRESIDENTIAL CANDIDATE. AND I'VE GOT A CASE OF POST-CONVENTION DOUBTS...

I MEAN..THE PRESIDENCY! WOW! LEADER OF THE FREE WORLD! GLOBAL DESTRUCTION AT HIS FINGERTIPS! AND WE NOMINATED A DEAD CAT! A DEAD CAT!! MY GOSH..MAYBE WE SHOULD HAVE FOUND SOMEONE WITH A MORE APPROPRIATE BACKGROUND! ...A MORE EXPERIENCED BACK-GROUND...

MILO!...WE SHOULD HAVE FOUND AN AMIABLE OLD EX-"B"MOVIE ACTOR!!

DON'T BE RIDICULOUS.

OH, MILO...WE SHOULD HAVE CALLED FRED MACMURRAY...

SO. WHADDYA SAY WE MELT ON OVER TO MY PLACE FOR A LITTLE OF THE OL' KOOTCHIE-KOO SKIDDOO?

UH...

GREAT, BABY. BUT FIRST I'D APPRECIATE YOU SIGNING THIS PRE-AFFAIR CONTRACT.

BESIDES ABSOLVING ME OF ALL EMOTIONAL COMMITMENT, IT MAKES YOU LIABLE FOR BROKEN FURNITURE, TORN CLOTHING, ½ THE COST OF MEALS AND ALL CAR REPAIRS WHEN YOU ROAR OFF IN A JEALOUS RAGE AND WRAP MY NEW CAMARO AROUND A TELEPHONE POLE.

DOES IT MAKE ME LIABLE FOR DENTAL WORK AFTER I KICK YOUR TEETH IN?

NO, BUT NOTE THE HERPES CLAUSE, HERE...

IF YOU PROMISE NOT TO TAKE ANY OF THIS PERSONALLY, I'LL READ YOU YOUR STANDING IN THE POLLS THIS MORNING...

GRUNT.

LESSEE...A "MINUS 17%." IN FACT, THEY SAY THAT FOR V.P., THE ONLY THING THAT THE AMERICAN PEOPLE WOULD PREFER LESS THAN YOURSELF IS...IS... UH...OH, DEAR...

SLURP.

...A CUCUMBER.

PPHWEPTH!

WOULD THEY HAVE TOLD LINCOLN AT 5:38 a.m. THAT HE WAS BARELY AHEAD OF A CUCUMBER IN THE POLLS? NO. ROOSEVELT? NO. TRUMAN? NO. CARTER? POSSIBLY BUT NOT NECESSARILY.

FRAZZLED
THE UGLY, SORDID LIFE, DEATH AND REBIRTH OF BILL THE CAT

BOB WOODWARD

EXCLUSIVE

THIS WEEK'S SERIALIZED INSTALLMENT:
"The Fall of a Giant"

SUNDAY, SEPTEMBER 9, 1983... THE COMICS PAGE OF THE L.A. HERALD EXAMINER. WEDGED BETWEEN "HI AND LOIS" AND "ZIGGY", A LIMP CAT LIES NEARLY COMA-TOSE. BILL HAD CHOSEN THE METHOD MOST POP-ULAR AMONG TODAY'S SUPERSTARS TO DEAL WITH SPECTACULAR SUCCESS: HE MELTED HIS BRAIN.

HMMPH! SNIFF! SNORT!

THE SAME DAY. WASHINGTON. THE SENATE/COMICS GUILD HEARINGS...

IT'S ALL A MEDIA MYTH, SENATOR. THERE IS NO MORE A DRUG PROBLEM IN THE CARTOON INDUSTRY THAN IN...OH...SAY, THE ENTERTAINMENT INDUSTRY.

WELL! THAT IS A RELIEF!

LATER, SOURCES CLOSE TO BILL WOULD ANONYMOUSLY RECOUNT THE GREAT CAT'S FINAL, SAD DAYS.

ONE DAY HE STARTED CHASING THE GIRLS AROUND THE POOL WITH A PAIR OF ICE TONGS, SCREAMING "PIRANHA!" HE WAS CLEARLY OUT OF CONTROL. THEN HE TOSSED ONE OF THE SWANS INTO THE JACUZZI. HEF NEVER LET BILL INTO THE MANSION AGAIN.

ONE NIGHT BILL SHOWED UP ABOUT 4:00 A.M. AT MY WEST HOLLYWOOD BUNGALOW. HE WAS WHACKED. A MOVIE DEAL JUST FELL THROUGH AND HE WAS UPSET, SO HE THREW A CINDER BLOCK THROUGH THE WIND-SHIELD OF MY NEW BMW 533. THEN HE DRANK ALL MY ROOT BEER, STOLE MY MERCEDES AND RAN OVER MY MITT. I NEVER SAW HIM ALIVE AGAIN. I'M VERY DEPRESSED ABOUT THIS.

ALL I KNOW IS THAT RIGHT BEFORE HE WAS KILLED, HE TOLD ME THAT HE BELIEVED HE WOULD COME BACK IN HIS SECOND LIFE AS SHIRLEY MacLAINE. YEP!... THE DRUGS HAD CLEARLY TAKEN THEIR TOLL. AND DON'T USE MY NAME WITH THIS!

NEXT WEEK... "THE FINAL 24 HOURS"

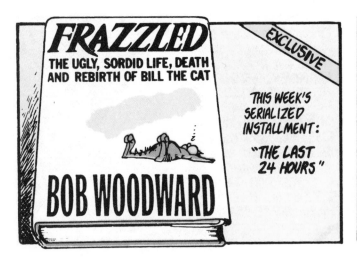

EXCLUSIVE

FRAZZLED

THE UGLY, SORDID LIFE, DEATH AND REBIRTH OF BILL THE CAT

BOB WOODWARD

THIS WEEK'S SERIALIZED INSTALLMENT:

"THE LAST 24 HOURS"

TUESDAY. SEPTEMBER 30TH. 7:16 a.m. A LATE-NIGHT PARTY IN COMIC STAR **MARY WORTH'S** LOS ANGELES HOME. BIG NAMES. BIG MONEY. BIG TEMPTATIONS... **BIG SINS**. IT FINALLY BREAKS UP WITH THE DAWN. "NEED A LIFT HOME?" ASKS SNUFFY SMITH. HE'S NOTICED BILL, WHO LOOKS BAD. "ACK," REPLIES THE CAT AND STUMBLES TOWARD HIS CAR. SMITH SHRUGS.

11:05 a.m. ROUTE 66. EAST TOWARD HOME. BILL'S NERVOUS SYSTEM—RAVAGED BY MONTHS OF CHEMICAL ABUSE—TEETERS PRECARIOUSLY ON THE BRINK OF TOTAL, CATASTROPHIC FAILURE...

SNORT!

HIGH NOON. THE OUTSKIRTS OF BLOOM COUNTY. 143 M.P.H. OBLIVION...DEAD AHEAD...THE PIPER IS ABOUT TO BE PAID...

VROOOM!! VROOOM!!

CACTUS AHEAD

SCREEEECH! oooo

7:43 p.m. A SCENE OF TOTAL AUTOMOTIVE DEVASTATION. A LONE AND SORROWFUL FIGURE DISCOVERS THAT OF THE ONCE GLORIOUS BILL THE CAT...NOT ONE SCRAP REMAINS. NOT ONE SINGLE, SOLITARY PIECE... EXCEPT...

GREAT SCOTT! IT'S HIS...HIS...

NEXT WEEK: THE SHOCKING SECRET

FRAZZLED
THE UGLY, SORDID LIFE, DEATH AND REBIRTH OF BILL THE CAT

BOB WOODWARD

STILL EXCLUSIVE

The Third and Hopefully Final Installment: "He Hath Risen Again"

IT WAS MILO BLOOM, FRIEND AND BUSINESS ASSOCIATE OF BILL THE CAT, WHO FIRST ARRIVED AT THE SCENE OF THE FIERY CAR CRASH. IT WAS ALSO HE WHO DISCOVERED THE ONLY INTACT PORTION OF THE ONCE GREAT ENTERTAINER WHICH REMAINED... HIS *TONGUE*.

HOW TOTALLY GROSS.

≡SNIFF!≡ HERE... TAKE IT, OLIVER WENDELL JONES...≡SOB!≡ I'M...I'M TOO STRICKEN WITH GRIEF... THIS IS ALL THAT'S LEFT OF BILL... PLEASE... GIVE HIM A NICE BURIAL OR SOMETHING...

OR SOMETHING.

Milo's Meat Wagon

...OR SOMETHING, INDEED! FOR THERE WERE STILL LIVING GENETIC THINGUMAJIGS AND DNA DOOHICKEYS IN THAT OL' TONGUE OF BILL'S! AND THUS BEGAN THE MOST DARING EXPERIMENT EVER TO BE CONDUCTED BEFORE BEDTIME... THE CLONING OF A CAT!

ACK!

JUNIOR Chemistry

THERE WERE, QUITE NATURALLY, SOME MINOR SETBACKS...

DRAT!

BUT THEN, SUCCESS! AND WHILE OLIVER W. JONES — SCIENTIST, HACKER AND MICHAEL JACKSON DETRACTOR — SLEPT EXHAUSTED, AN UNKNOWING WORLD MOURNED A SOUL WHO HAD FILLED THE LIVES OF MILLIONS WITH HOPE, JOY AND CAT SPITTLE... A SOUL WHO HAD ALSO... *RETURNED!*

ACK YECH BARF SNORT

12:40 a.m.. Clear sky. 72°. The moon's third quadrant is visible ...

...as are the ice particles in Saturn's inner rings. —Simply fabulous!

Erupting hydrogen geysers are clearly visible on Cygnus Four's third planet while its sister star appears to be collapsing upon itself!..

Focusing deeper, beta explosions can be seen near the Aurorus Galaxy, while Romulan attack ships are burning and adrift off the great ion fields of Sirius Six !!

..and there !! a black hole is clearly drawing off stellar material from Alpha Seven ! A fantastic cosmic whirlpool sucking the nearby planets into an unimaginable maelstrom of frozen time, twisted reality and unexplored **dimensions!!**

Meanwhile, Edna-Mae Fernbugle is still picking her toes and watching "Dick Clark's Celebrity Bloopers."

The Merry Meadow Players present

"A FEW MOMENTS AT THE NATIONAL ORGANIZATION OF LIBERATED MEN"

Cast:

The Chairman....Mr. M. Bloom
Ralph...........Mr. P. Opus
Frank...........Mr. Portnoy

Directed by Milo Bloom
Set Design by M. Binkley

...AT 6:00, THERE'LL BE A TALK ON "WHY MEN DON'T TOUCH"... AND AT 6:30... "IS 'MACHO' JUST A HORMONE PROBLEM?"

UH.. SAY, RALPH...YOU LOOK TROUBLED...DO YOU WISH TO SHARE YOUR FEELINGS WITH THE REST OF US?

NO! THAT'S OKAY!

RALPHIE...WE'RE ALL SENSITIVE, CARING BEINGS HERE...LET YOUR EMOTIONS FLOW!

OKAY.

WELL...IT'S MY WIFE... SHE CAUGHT ME READING A "LADIES' HOME JOURNAL" YESTERDAY... I EXPLAINED I WAS ONLY TRYING TO FIND A WAY TO GET THOSE AWFUL SMUDGES OFF THE END TABLE...AND THEN SHE CALLED ME A...A...

..."A WIMP!! SOB

GOOD! THAT'S GOOD! FREE YOUR FEELINGS! ...OH, FRANK? WOULD YOU COME UP HERE AND GIVE RALPH A "REASSURANCE HUG"?

SURE!

CONTINUING... AT 7:30, I'LL BE GIVING A LECTURE ON "THE IMAGE OF MEN IN AMERICA: STALE ROLES AND TIGHT BUNS"...

HOLD ME, FRANK!   I'M HERE RALPH!

♪♪♪♪♪

OH. YES... HELLO! WELCOME TO THE AMERICAN MEADOW PARTY'S FIRST AND ONLY POLITICAL COMMERCIAL ... ON WHICH, I'M TOLD, WE'VE BLOWN ALL OF OUR REMAINING DOUGH.

AHEM. WE OFFER NO WILD PROMISES. WE ONLY OFFER OURSELVES. BILL, HERE, IS A FORMER MISSIONARY. I AM STUDYING TO BE THE POPE. OUR VALUES ARE SUPERB. WE WANT YOUR VOTE.

SOME SAY WE'RE DESPERATE. NOT TRUE! WE PLEDGE NEVER TO STOOP TO UNSAVORY PETTY POLITICKING WITH THE TWO FRONTRUNNERS...

NAMELY, THE DEMOCRATIC CANDIDATE, SEEN HERE IN A 1972 PHOTO WITH MADALYN MURRAY O'HAIR AT AN "UP WITH ATHEISTS" BANQUET...

...AND THE REPUBLICAN CANDIDATE, SEEN HERE IN A 1959 PHOTO SHARING A SMOKE AND REMINISCING WITH ROOMMATE AND FORMER FRAT BROTHER FIDEL "STOGIE" CASTRO.

AND SO NEXT TUESDAY, THINK OF US... AND THINK OF THEM. THE "BEAK AND SALIVA TICKET..." GO FOR IT! THANK YOU.

♪♪♪♪♪

PH-ZZZZ..
=CRACKLE=

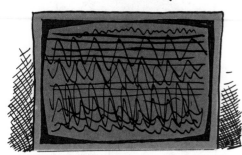

WE INTERRUPT THIS PROGRAM FOR A SPECIAL MESSAGE FROM THE UNITED STATES FEDERAL ELECTION COMMISSION...

ON OCTOBER 28TH, THE AMERICAN MEADOW PARTY BROADCAST A PAID POLITICAL COMMERCIAL NARRATED BY THEIR V.P. CANDIDATE SHOWN HERE.

GULP!

POLITICAL DISTORTIONIST

THE COMMERCIAL INCLUDED TWO PHOTO-GRAPHS APPARENTLY SHOWING RONALD REAGAN AND WALTER MONDALE IN CLOSE ASSOCIATION WITH FIDEL CASTRO AND MADALYN MURRAY O'HAIR, RESPECTIVELY.

I'M NOT RESPONSIBLE! REALLY!

THE COMMISSION HAS LEARNED THAT THE PHOTOS HAD BEEN TAMPERED WITH.

THEM! THEY MADE ME DO IT! MY ADVISORS! THEM! THEM!

THE FOLLOWING ARE THE GENUINE, UN-DOCTORED PHOTOS WHICH CLEARLY SHOW WHO THE CANDIDATES WERE ACTUALLY APPEARING WITH...

"BULLWINKLE..."

AND "PUGSLEY" FROM "THE ADDAMS FAMILY".

WE HOPE THOSE RESPONSIBLE FULLY REALIZE JUST EXACTLY HOW MUCH TROUBLE THEY'RE IN.

OH, THEY DO, MAN, THEY DO!

POLITICAL

ELECTION DAY. I'M A NERVOUS WRECK...THIS..? THIS IS POLITICS?..

Vote BILL N'OPUS FOR A WEIRDER AMERICA

...WE'RE DEAD IN THE POLLS... ANOTHER BABY PIDDLED ON MY TIE IN FRONT OF THE MEDIA... AND GEORGE WILL REFERRED TO ME AS AN "OBSEQUIOUS LIBERAL PEON".

BY GOLLY, ONE MORE LITTLE POLITICAL SETBACK AND I...I'M HEADING FOR TIMBUKTU!!

YOUR RUNNING MATE JUST RAN OFF TO BE A "RAJNEESHEE" CULTIST.

WONDERFUL. GOOD-BYE.

VICTORY

GOOD MORNIN AMERICA

NEXT STOP: ☆ THE WHITE HOUSE! ☆

DID YOU WIN?

NO, I DO NOT THINK WE SHOULD LET BILL THE CAT "ROT WITH THE RAJNEESHEES". I THINK WE SHOULD RESCUE THE LITTLE FELLOW...

JUST IMAGINE HIM RIGHT NOW...SITTING AROUND IN A PINK TUNIC...BRAINWASHED... CHANTING INCOMPREHENSIBLY...

EATING SOY CAKES... WEAVING RUGS...

...WRITING CHECKS TO THE "BHAGWAN" FROM OUR CAMPAIGN FUND...

BY GOD, WE'VE GOT TO RESCUE THAT POOR BOY.

UP! UP! WAKE UP, OPUS!

C'MON... OPEN THEM BABY BLUES... WE HAVE A JOB TO DO...

SLAP! SLAP!

YOU AND I ARE DRIVING TO OREGON, WHERE WE WILL RAID THE RAJNEESHEE CULT AND DARINGLY KIDNAP BILL THE CAT, RETURNING HIM BACK HOME SAFELY IN TIME FOR CHRISTMAS. NOW GO WASH UP!

THIS SOUNDS LIKE A HORRIBLE TV MOVIE STARRING "MR. T" AND BERT CONVY.

I MUST SAY... CULT OR NO CULT, GETTING BACK OUT ON THE OPEN ROAD AGAIN IS INVIGORATING.

♫ OH, I'M ON THAT LONG ROAD TO TUSCALOO WITH MY FAT BABY CARMALOU... ♫

PLEASE EXCUSE ME. THE FREEDOM OF THE HIGHWAY AND THE RUSH OF THE WIND OFTEN MAKES ME A LITTLE GIDDY.

GOOD. YOU CAN BACK OUT OF THE GARAGE NOW.

MOVIN' OUT!

OKAY. WE'RE HERE. AND THERE'S THE RAJNEESHEES. NOW GO IN THERE, MINGLE AND GRAB OUR POOR BILL THE CAT.

OH MY. OH DEAR.

WELCOME TO ANTELOPE RAJNEESH

GULP!

IF, SEVERAL YEARS FROM NOW, YOU FIND ME IN AN AIRPORT SELLING PETUNIAS AND LOOKING LOBOTOMIZED, I'D APPRECIATE YOUR STRANGLING ME.

SAY, BROTHER...UH, HOW ABOUT REFRESHING ME ON THIS RAJNEESH BUSINESS...

HAPPY PEAS

WELL, RAJNEESH IS THE TRUTH.. AND THE TRUTH IS THE LIGHT.. WHICH IS LIFE. LIFE'S TRUTH LIGHT. AND HAPPINESS. WHICH IS WEARING RED PAJAMAS AND BLOWING KISSES TOWARD THE BHAGWAN'S 72 GOLD ROLLS-ROYCES.

WHOA! BY GOLLY...THAT DOES MAKE A LOT OF SENS--

PSST! OPUS! SNAP OUT OF IT!!

≈PANT! PANT!≈ WELL YOU HAVE TO ADMIT... ≈PANT! PANT!≈ THAT'S A FRIGHTEN-INGLY SEDUCTIVE PHILOSOPHY!!

THE CABIN OF BHAGWAN BILL

NO CHANTING

THE CABIN OF BHAGWAN BILL

OOF! ≈GRUNT!≈ OUCH!

THE CABIN OF BHAGWAN BILL

NO CHANTING

ACKMMPH!

START THE CAR!!

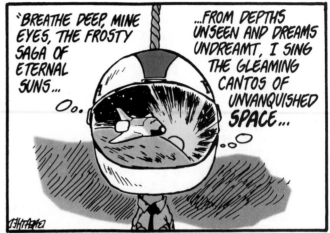

114

WHAT ARE YOU DOING?

ME? OH, I'M JUST HANGIN' OUT.

YOU'RE HOPING YOUR MOTHER WILL CALL AND WISH YOU A MERRY CHRISTMAS, AREN'T YOU?

I NEVER SAID THAT!

OPUS, YOUR MOTHER ABANDONED YOU ON AN ICE FLOE SIX YEARS AGO. SHE'S A FLOOZY...ADDICTED TO FERMENTED HERRING JUICE. SHE'S PROBABLY DANCING IN GIN JOINTS THROUGHOUT SOUTH AMERICA. NOW LET'S FACE REALITY, SHALL WE?

AND A HAPPY NEW YEAR TO YOU, TOO!!

DID YOUR MOTHER NEGLECT TO SEND YOU A CARD AGAIN THIS YEAR?

P. OPUS

ME?..WHY..WHY NO... THIS IS HERS RIGHT HERE! YES! THE 2ND ONE THIS WEEK... THE 3RD TODAY, IN FACT!...

..PROOF POSITIVE, I MIGHT ADD, THAT I HAVE THE WORLD'S MOST LOVING AND COMPASSIONATE MOTHER...CONTRARY TO POPULAR RUMOR! SO THERE! THPPTHP!!

Dear Occupant,

THE HOLIDAYS ARE HARDLY A TIME OF JOY FOR THOSE OF US WITH DELINQUENT MOTHERS.

LO, I AM DEPRESSED, DISHEARTENED... NAY, DISMAYED.

MIGHT THERE BE SOMEONE ELSE OUT THERE WHO'S AS DEEPLY IN THE DUMPS AS ME ON THIS BRIGHT CHRISTMAS MORN??...

SOME ASSEMBLY REQUIRED

BANANA PC JUNIOR 6000 SERIES COMPUTER

THE "BANANA JUNIOR" 6000 SERIES. 32 BIT. 450 K. TRULY, A STATE-OF-THE-ART MACHINE.

≥BEEP!≤

TIME FOR A NUTRITIONAL INTERLUDE.

BUT CAN IT BALANCE A CHECKBOOK?

YUCK. THE FRITOS ARE ANTIQUATED.

"WELCOME TO THE WONDERFUL WORLD OF YOUR NEW 'BANANA JUNIOR 6000 SERIES FULLY PORTABLE PERSONAL COMPUTER'".

THIS ONE DOES IT ALL! COMPUTES! SORTS! PRINTS! DRAWS! FIGURES! DOODLES! SLICES! DICES! WHISTLES! WHIMPERS! DANCES! PRANCES!...

I.B.M. SUCKS SILICON

..AND MOST IMPORTANT OF ALL...

DOINK! POINK! POINK!

WHOA! HE'S HOT!

BANANA JUNIOR

.. IT TURNS OFF."

CLICK!

SHWUNK!

YET ANOTHER SAD EXAMPLE OF TODAY'S COMMON MAN TRYING FUTILELY TO KEEP PACE WITH THE SPEEDING TECHNOLOGY.

I'M SORRY. I'M A LITTLE EXCITED. AWFUL JOKE. I BEG YOUR PARDON.

..TODAY'S GUEST IS MR. ROLAND. HE'S A PAINTER. CAN YOU SAY "PAINTER"?

"RHINOCEROS"

GOOD! I KNEW YOU COULD!

!

MR. ROLAND PAINTS CARS. CAN YOU SAY "CAR"?

"TED KOPPEL IS A WAFFLE"

GOOD!

MISTER ROGERS HAS GONE BANANAS!

MILO! PER CHANCE, HAVE YOU SEEN MY "BANANA JR." CRUISE BY?

YES. IT SEEMED TO BE HEADED FOR STEVE DALLAS' PLACE.

STEVE DALLAS!? HOLY MODEMS! HE'LL TAKE AN AX TO IT!

NONSENSE.

..I DON'T THINK VIOLENCE IS WHAT'S ON STEVE'S MIND RIGHT NOW.

NEW YEAR

1985

...CHARLENE?

1985

CHARLENE... HONEY BABE... I THOUGHT YOU LEFT. HOW 'BOUT TIP-TOEIN' THROUGH MY TULIPS?

OH, MAMA, YOU DO KNOW WHAT I LIKE! A LITTLE HIGHER, PLEASE..

POINK! POINK!

NOW COME ON OVER AND PLANT THOSE BIG RUBY REDS RIGHT **HERE**....

DID YOU HEAR THAT SCREAM?! SOUNDED LIKE...LIKE...

...SOMEBODY WITH HIS LIPS CAUGHT IN A DISK DRIVE!

STEVE?

I'M IN HERE! I'VE GOT THIS SAVAGE HORROR CORNERED!!

MY GOD..THIS THING TRIED TO SUCK MY LIPS OFF! IS IT REAL OR AM I SUFFERING SOME SATANIC POST-HOLIDAY TEQUILA HALLUCINATION?

IT'S REAL.

SMALL RELIEF. GET IT OUT OF HERE.

WE'RE GOING.

AND TAKE THOSE SIXTEEN ★●#✱?! ELVES WITH YOU!

HELLO? BANANA ELECTRONICS, INC.? I'M HAVING TROUBLE WITH MY NEW "BANANA JR." PERSONAL COMPUTER.

WHAT'S THE PROBLEM?

HE KEEPS SPITTING OUT MY CHEAP SOFTWARE.

DID YOU TELL HIM WHERE WE'D PUT HIS PRIMARY MEMORY CHIPS IF HE WAS RETURNED?

NOT EXACTLY.

PUT HIM ON THE PHONE.

OH, GOSH..

TOASTER OVENS! DID YOU HEAR ME?... PROGRAMMABLE TOASTER OVENS!

WHOA.

THAT'S IT. LET'S HAVE IT, OPUS.

GO AWAY! I'M STILL A NATIONAL CANDIDATE.

YOU **LOST**. YOUR PUBLIC USEFULNESS HAS EXPIRED. TIME TO RETIRE PAINFUL SYMBOLS OF DEFEATED IDEALS.

NO! I WILL **NOT** BE PUT OUT TO POLITICAL PASTURE!!

GRAB IT, BOYS!! AAAIGH!!

WE SHALL BURY IT WITH THE SNAILS.

THEY SENT FERRARO OUT ON THE LECTURE CIRCUIT, YA KNOW!

120

LIFE. IT'S LIKE...A BLUSTERY DAY...THROWING ITS WINDS OF TROUBLE AND TRAVAIL RIGHT INTO OUR FACES...

LEAVING US TO LEAN INTO OUR PAINFUL DESTINIES... FARTHER AND FARTHER...

..AND EVEN FARTHER ...

..UNTIL AN OTHERWISE PROMISING ANALOGY IS HOPELESSLY SHOT AND WE'RE SNORTING SOD.

SO THERE I WAS AGAIN ON THAT BLEAK, MIDNIGHT THRESHOLD OF MY HORRID ANXIETY CLOSET...

FOR AT 8 YEARS AND 4 MONTHS OF AGE, THE SITUATION HAD BECOME CRITICAL ...

...AFTER FALLING POPULARITY AT SCHOOL AND GENERALLY POOR REVIEWS AT HOME..THE SITUATION WAS FRIGHTENINGLY CLEAR..

..MY RATINGS WERE IN THE DUMPS.

I'M SORRY. WE'RE CANCELING YOUR CHILDHOOD.

YOU'RE CANCELING MY CHILD-HOOD?!

HEY! BINKLEY BABE! ALL OF US UP IN THE EXECUTIVE OFFICES ARE MAD ABOUT YOU.. REALLY...BUT THE NIELSENS CAME OUT TODAY. NOT GOOD, BABE.

YOU CAN'T RATE A LIFE LIKE A TV SHOW !...

YER DOWN 20 POINTS WITH TEACHERS..DOWN 13 WITH FRIENDS AND 9 WITH FAMILY. OUCH, BABE!

SORRY GUY. YER JUST NOT BRINGIN' IN THE BIG NUMBERS..."BIG-MOUTHED". "PRECOCIOUS"... THAT'S WHAT I'VE BEEN HEARING..

WELL, THEY HAVEN'T CANCELED GARY COLEMAN !

THAT LITTLE MIDGET'S GOT A 90-YEAR CONTRACT. I THROW UP JUST THINKIN' ABOUT IT.

HE WAS GONE. BACK UP TO THE CORPORATE OFFICES WHENCE HE CAME. BUT HE, THE CHIEF PRO-GRAMMER, HAD RENEWED ME FOR ANOTHER SEASON..

YES, WITH BETTER CHARACTER DEVELOPMENT AND A MORE MEANINGFUL PLOT LINE, MY LIFE WOULD BE GUARANTEED AN EXTENDED RUN.

BUT QUALITY HAD TO BE MAIN-TAINED, HE SAID..OR ELSE! OR ELSE WHAT ? I ASKED... OR ELSE THE EVIL..THE UNHOLY.. THE UNSPEAKABLE WOULD BE ORDERED UPON ME ...

..A LAUGH TRACK !

THE HORROR... THE HORROR!

GENE SIMMONS NEVER HAD A PERSONAL COMPUTER WHEN HE WAS A KID

How do we know? We know because our own well-documented research has shown conclusively that a child who lacks his own personal computer during those earliest school years will very probably grow up to be a bass player in a heavy-metal rock band who wears women's fishnet pantyhose and sticks his tongue down to his kneecaps. Just like Gene Simmons.

Your child's future doesn't have to look like this. The Banana Junior 6000 Self-portable Personal Computer System, complete with its optional soft-

ware— Bananawrite, Bananadraw, Bananafile and Bananamanager—is just what your four-year-old needs to compete in today's cut-throat world of high tech and high expectations.

The Banana Junior 6000....
Buy one before it's too late.
Gene's mother wishes she had.

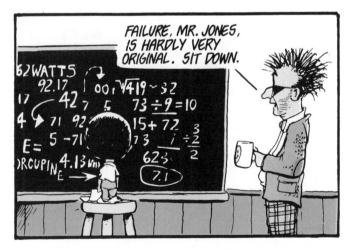

THIS IS ADAM 13.. SEND AN AMBULANCE TO MAIN AND GILBERT. WE'VE GOT SIX ASSAULT VICTIMS HERE..

MAN! SOMEBODY MUSTA JUST GONE BERSERK!

ARE THEY ALIVE?

BARELY. IT LOOKS LIKE THESE PUNKS PICKED THE WRONG GUY TO HARASS THIS TIME.

VIGILANTE, EH? WHAT DID HE BEAT THEM WITH?

≥SNIFF!≤ SMELLS LIKE.. ≥SNIFF!≤ A BIG SLAB OF OLIVE LOAF...

THE BLOOM Beacon
"OLIVE-LOAF VIGILANTE" PUMMELS STREET MIMES
★ HUNDREDS CALL POLICE PRAISING MYSTERY MAN
★ UNLICENSED LUNCHEON MEAT WAS WEAPON

I S'POSE YOU'VE HEARD ABOUT THE VIGILANTE... WHACKIN' THOSE STREET MIMES WITH AN OLIVE LOAF LAST NIGHT...

SUCH A STORY IT IS! SUCH A TRAGIC AND VIOLENT STORY IT IS INDEED!

GOODNESS ONLY KNOWS WHAT SCURRILOUS FORCES ARE MOBILIZING AT THIS VERY MOMENT TO EXPLOIT THE WHOLE SORRY AFFAIR...

FALL IN!! A BLATT! BLATT!! BLATT!!!

The Bloom Beacon

MOVE IT, PEOPLE! WE'VE GOT A VIGILANTE OUT THERE BOPPING STREET PERFORMERS! I WANT RUMORS! DIRT! SCANDAL! TITILLATING PERSONAL DETAILS!

The Bloom Beacon

CITY DESK

HELLO? EDITORIALS? I WANT INDIGNATION.. SHOCK...MORAL OUTRAGE. THIS IS NO WAY A CIVILIZED SOCIETY SHOULD DEAL WITH ITS UNSAVORY ELEMENTS.

The Bloom Beacon

CITY DESK

NEWS!. GIVE ME A 20-INCH HEADLINE: "MYSTERY MAN MUGS MIMES WITH MEAT—MILLIONS MAKE MERRY!"

The Bloom Beacon

CITY DESK

BAD NEWSPAPERS LIVE FOR THIS KIND OF THING.

The Bloom Beacon

CITY DESK

WHO'LL JOIN ME IN A TOAST TO THE "OLIVE-LOAF VIGILANTE"?.. HERO FOR THE COMMON MAN!

I WILL!.. GOD BLESS HIM!

HEY..IF THE POLICE CAN'T EVEN PROTECT US FROM THE MUGGERS AND RAPISTS, HOW THE HELL CAN THEY PROTECT US FROM THE STREET MIMES?!

LADY, YOU ARE RIGHT!

AND IF NOT THE STREET MIMES, HOW SAFE ARE WE FROM...FROM THE LAWYERS?!

YEAH!

SHOOT THE ★@#?!★ LAWYERS!!

LADY, YOU ARE TANKED.

TODAY, WITNESSES DESCRIBED THE "OLIVE-LOAF VIGILANTE" AS BEING THREE FEET TALL, WITH A HUGE NOSE AND WEARING WHAT APPEARED TO BE A TUXEDO...

..A ROUGH POLICE SKETCH WAS QUICKLY MADE AND DISTRIBUTED TO THE MEDIA...

POLICE SKETCH

UH OH.

DR. JOYCE BROTHERS... GIVE US, PLEASE, THE PSYCHOLOGICAL PROFILE OF THE MYSTERY VIGILANTE.

CERTAINLY...

SELF-ASSURED. FORCEFUL. HE MATCHES HIS RAGING VIOLENCE INFLICTED UPON SOCIETY'S EVIL DEVIANTS WITH EQUALLY RAGING PASSION SHOWN TOWARD HIS WOMEN..

THIS PERSON...THIS ANGRY MAN-BEAST OF VENGEANCE...WHEREVER HE IS HIDING, REMAINS A SEETHING, CHURNING VOLCANO OF PRIMAL HATE/LUST...

I KNOW YOU'RE IN THERE, OPUS. I ALSO KNOW YOU'RE THE MYSTERY VIGILANTE. COME ON OUT. OPUS?

HEY! YA WANNA GO TO JAIL?..IS THAT WHAT YA WANT? YA WANNA GET LOCKED UP WITH RAPISTS, MURDERERS AND POPE ABUSERS?...

WELL I CAN'T HELP IF YA DON'T COME OUT. HELLO?

AWRIGHT. IF THAT'S HOW YOU'RE GONNA--

POPE ABUSERS?

BINKLEY! DISASTER! THEY JUST ARRESTED OPUS! TOOK HIM AWAY IN CHAINS! RIGHT!

LISTEN..TRY TO FIND STEVE DALLAS...HE'S GONNA NEED A LAWYER.. EVEN A ROTTEN ONE.

OH, THIS IS AWFUL! OPUS JUST CAN'T DEAL WITH BEING IN JAIL...

I SAID TRY IT AGAIN!

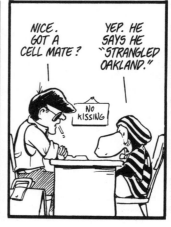

YOU ARE A FINE AND NOBLE FATHER AND YOUR SON LOVES YOU IMMENSELY.

I HAD AN ANXIETY ATTACK. WHAT IF YOU DIED TONIGHT AND I HADN'T MADE SURE YOU KNEW JUST HOW MUCH YOU MEAN TO ME?

SO I WENT OUT AND BOUGHT YOU A TOKEN GIFT.. A SYMBOLIC GESTURE TO REASSURE YOU OF YOUR SON'S ETERNAL LOVE.

"BAWDY BABES AND LUSTY LASSES"

THERE'S NOT MUCH OPEN AT 4 A.M..

C'MON... JUST ONE HINT! I WON'T TELL! IS IT BIGGER THAN A BREAD BOX?

NO COMMENT!

WAIT... LEMME GUESS.. IS IT THE PENTAGON'S LAUNDRY?

NO COMMENT!

NASA LOVES TO PLAY "GUESS WHAT WE'RE SHIPPING UP IN THE NEXT SECRET SHUTTLE FLIGHT"!

IS IT "THE LENNON SISTERS"?

NO!

CONGRATULATIONS, MR. JONES, ON YOUR AWARD-WINNING NUCLEAR BOMB MODEL.

IT'S NO MODEL. IT WORKS!

REALLY. AND WHERE DID YOU GET THE RADIOACTIVE MATERIAL?

I SCRAPED THE LUMINOUS STUFF OFF 9,700 OLD GLOW-IN-THE-DARK WATCH HANDS.

REALLY.

REALLY. KABOOM!

OKAY, PEOPLE.. FIRE DRILL!

CLAP! CLAP!

COOL YOUR JETS. I GOT THE SAFETY ON.

WELL, THIS IS SIMPLY A SCANDAL. STRIPPED OF MY AWARD AND BANISHED TO MY ROOM FOR THE CRIME OF BRINGING A NUCLEAR WEAPON TO SCHOOL...

DO THEY THINK MY SCIENTIFIC PRIDE ISN'T CRUSHED? DO THEY THINK I'M NOT HURT?

WELL I AM FLESH AND BLOOD!...NOT JUST A CALCULATING JUMBLE OF COLD AND UNFEELING WIRES AND CIRCUITS.

NO OFFENSE.

NONE TAKEN.

132

WHAT?

OH, NOTHING.

EVER FEEL LIKE DOING SOMETHING ENTIRELY AGAINST YOUR NATURE AND WHACKING A GOOFY SMILE RIGHT IN THE TEETH?

WHAT?

OH, NOTHING.

WHATTSA MATTER, CHIEF?

TENSE... FRUSTRATED... THE PUBLIC HATES US...THE STAFF KEEPS SPELLING "ALL RIGHT" AS ONE WORD...

EDITOR DO NOT HASSLE

YEAH...IT'S ROUGH AT THE TOP, BOSS. YA NEED A BREAK... DO SOMETHING SILLY AND FUN...

DO SOMETHING WHICH THOSE IN YOUR POSITION USUALLY ONLY DREAM OF...

EDITOR DO NOT HASSLE

GO BEAT THE CARTOONIST.

YEAH...

EDITOR DO NOT HASSLE

SPRING MUST BE HERE...CAN YOU SMELL WHAT'S IN THE AIR, OPUS?

THAT'S RIGHT... GO AHEAD AND MOCK ME!

OKAY! SO MAYBE I'M NOT THAT FREQUENTLY BLESSED WITH FEMALE ATTENTION! MAYBE I DON'T HAVE THE RAW SEXUAL MAGNETISM OF A DAVID LETTERMAN...

BUT I, TOO, SMELL LOVE IN THE AIR IN SPRING... AND I DON'T NEED ANYONE ELSE TO REMIND ME THAT I SMELL LOVE IN THE AIR IN SPRING!

OH, WHY DO YOU ALL TORTURE ME SO?

ALL I SMELLED WAS MILDEW..

"HE WAS AWAKE A LONG TIME BEFORE HE REMEMBERED THAT HIS HEART WAS BROKEN."

HEMINGWAY WROTE IT. I FEAR THAT THAT IS MY ROMANTIC DESTINY: TO BE A BROKEN-HEARTED IDIOT.

NEVERTHELESS.. IT IS TIME FOR ME AND MY HORMONES TO SEEK APPROPRIATE FEMININE FELLOWSHIP.

SON, YOU HAVEN'T THE CASH FOR A FLING.

SIR! MONEY CAN NOT BUY LOVE..

NO, BUT IT IMPROVES YOUR BARGAINING POSITION. HERE'S TEN BUCKS.

CHIEF..WE'VE GOT A PROBLEM WITH OUR "PERSONALS" EDITOR.

EDITOR DO NOT HASSLE

I HAPPEN TO KNOW THAT HE'S GOING THROUGH A DIFFICULT, DESPERATE PHASE OF HIS LIFE RIGHT NOW...

EDITOR DO NOT HASSLE

AND I FEAR THAT HIS JOURNALISTIC OBJECTIVITY IS SUFFERING JUST A TAD...

EDITOR DO NOT HASSLE

"WOMAN, 37, SEEKS SINCERE--"

TAKE ME.

PERSONALS Dept.

I'M ON MY LUNCH BREAK. I'D LIKE TO PLACE A "PERSONAL AD" PLEASE.

PERSONALS Dept.

"WOMAN, 26, SEEKS MAN. MUST BE BIG AND DUMB."

PERSONALS Dept

"BIG AND DUMB"?

RIGHT. NO ALAN ALDA - DONAHUE WIMPS. THANK GOD WE'RE OUT OF THE 70'S, DON'T YOU THINK?

PERSONALS Dept.

UH..

"BIG AND DUMB." I'M TALKIN' "JETHRO CLAMPETT."

PERSONALS Dept

ATTENTION! TODAY IS THURSDAY AND MISTER MICHAEL BINKLEY IS IN A FOUL AND UGLY MOOD.

THE GRASS LOOKS UGLY. THE FLOWERS SMELL UGLY. THE WHOLE DAY IS UGLY.

IN FACT, LIFE ITSELF IS LOOKING PRETTY MEANINGLESS IF NOT OUTRIGHT UGLY.

"HILL STREET BLUES" INTO RERUNS AGAIN?

YES.

SIR..I'VE BECOME INVOLVED WITH A WOMAN. THUS, I...I MUST RESIGN MY POSITION.

CITY DESK

MY FOCUS HAS CHANGED... MY PRIORITIES, SHIFTED... MY ORDERLY WORLD HAS JOYOUSLY BEEN TURNED ON ITS HEAD...

IN SHORT, THE DANDELIONS OF MY LIFE HAVE BEEN RUFFLED BY LOVE..AND I STAND NAKED, YET JUBILANT, FACING A BRIGHT, NEW DAWN!!

CITY DESK

"THE DANDELIONS OF HIS--"?

CAN YOU KEEP MY JOB OPEN IN CASE THINGS DON'T WORK OUT?

CITY DESK

YAWN.

AAIIGH!!

MY GOODNESS! FOR A MINUTE I THOUGHT I WAS TOM SELLECK AND COULDN'T FIGURE OUT HOW I SUDDENLY GOT SO DARNED UGLY!

WHAT AN INFINITELY DEPRESSING INCIDENT.

AH...THE AIR! TODAY THE AIR SMELLS SO...SO AIRY!

ISN'T THE GRASS LOOKING ESPECIALLY LOVELY TODAY? AND THE ROCKS!...SO... SO BEAUTIFULLY SCULPTED!... SO..SO NICELY SHAPED!

WHAT'S WRONG WITH YOU?

LOVE! I'M IN LOVE! IT CHANGES ONE'S OUTLOOK ON THE WORLD!

SO DOES DRINKING MOLDY EGGNOG.

LOOK! ASPHALT!

MADAM... I..HAVE A DATE. AND I AM IN NEED OF AN ODOR!

NOT JUST ANY ODOR, MIND YOU...BUT AN ODOR THAT'S ME! AN ODOR THAT SEZ I'M A 1985 AMERICAN MALE!!

I WANT AN ODOR THAT SEZ I CAN SPIT TOBACCO JUICE INTO WALTER "WIMP" MONDALE'S BREAST POCKET FROM FIFTY FEET WHILE CURSING THE SANDINISTAS AND MANHANDLING "MADONNA" ALL AT THE SAME TIME!!

WELL HERE'S A NICE--

JUST A PINT OF HORSE SWEAT, THANK YOU MA'AM.

YAWN.

PAD PAD PAD PAD

JUMPIN' JEHOSAPHAT!! I MUST'VE SLEPT ON MY HONKER WRONG! AND ME WITH A HOT DATE TONIGHT!

OOF! GRUNT! ARGH! ...OOF!

DON'T LAUGH. WAIT TILL THIS HAPPENS TO YOU.

WELL? TIME FOR MY DATE! HOW DO I LOOK?

UH... SOMETHING'S WRONG. WHAT'S WRONG?? MY SOCKS SMELL?

NO, NO... EVERYTHING'S FINE.. NO IT ISN'T! IT'S MY FACE, ISN'T IT?! THE "CLEARASIL" IS SHOWING, RIGHT?!

I DIDN'T SAY THAT... BINKLEY, YOU SAID THIS WAS INVISIBLE FLESH TONE!

OLIVER! LISTEN...OPUS HAS A DATE TONIGHT AND HE GOT HOLD OF A CAR, SOMEHOW! NO, NO!... DON'T PANIC! JUST ALERT THE LOCAL CIVIL DEFENSE! RIGHT! HURRY!

VROOOOM!! SQUACK! HONK! HONK! HONK! HONK! AAAIGPH... STOP YIKES!

Herbert for PRESIDENT

GREETINGS! I AM FANNIE LOU'S BEAU FOR THE EVENING! WILL YOU FETCH HER, PLEASE?

FANNIE LOU RAN OFF AND MARRIED A WRESTLER NAMED "SNAKE SMITH" IN LAS VEGAS YESTERDAY.

AS HER ROOMMATE, I'VE BEEN ASKED TO FILL IN. TAKE NOTE THAT I LOATHE ALL MEN. I'LL BE OUT IN A MINUTE, SLIME-FACE.

YESSIR...I JUST LIVE FOR LIFE'S LITTLE ROMANTIC SURPRISES!

MY NAME IS ALF MUSHPIE. LET'S GET THINGS UNDERSTOOD FOR THIS DATE...

I DON'T LIKE MEN. I DON'T LIKE MEN AT ALL. I DON'T LIKE MEN EVEN A TEENSY WEENSY BIT.

IN FACT, SOME OF US CONSIDER THE MALE OF THE SPECIES JUST ONE BIG, UGLY BRUTISH ABERRATION OF EVOLUTION.

OKAY. LET'S GO. I'M NOT GETTING ANY HICKIES TONIGHT, AM I?

I DUNNO, PORTNOY... I JUST THINK CUTTING YOUR HAIR LIKE **BILLY IDOL** WOULD BE FOOLISH.

FOOLISH? HEY! SIMPLY **EVERYBODY** IS DOING IT!

EXCUSE ME. MAY I INTERJECT WITH A HELPFUL PARABLE ON **FOOLISHNESS?**

WHEN I WAS JUST A LAD IN THE FALKLAND ISLANDS, WE WOULD ALL GATHER ON THE BEACH AND WATCH THE BRITISH JETS FLY PAST. SOMETIMES THEY WOULD GO BY ON THE LEFT...

...AND TWO MILLION PENGUINS WOULD SLOWLY TURN THEIR HEADS IN UNISON WATCHING THEM GO BY...

...AND THEN THEY'D TURN AROUND AND FLY BACK AND WE'D SLOWLY TURN OUR HEADS THE OTHER WAY...

..AND THEN THEY'D GO OUT TO SEA, TURN AROUND, AND COME IN RIGHT OVER US... HEADS GO UP... UP... UP... UP...

...AND TWO MILLION PENGUINS FALL OVER GENTLY ONTO THEIR BACKS.

WHAT'S THE MORAL?

"IF TWO MILLION PEOPLE DO A FOOLISH THING, IT IS **STILL** A FOOLISH THING."

HOW ABOUT THIS: "OPUS IS A YOGURT HEAD."

THPTPH!

WHILE THE MASTER PARABLE-TELLER LIES MORTALLY INSULTED, HE WONDERS HOW HE EVER EXPECTED TO ESTABLISH A MORAL LINK BETWEEN BILLY IDOL AND PENGUINS. MEANWHILE, THE WORLD TURNS FOOLISHLY ON AND ANTS TICKLE HIS BUTT.

141

KNOCK! KNOCK! KNOCK!

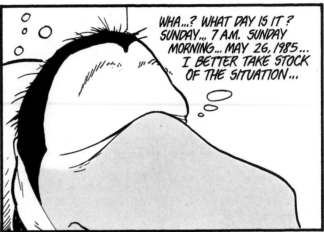

WHA...? WHAT DAY IS IT? SUNDAY... 7 A.M. SUNDAY MORNING... MAY 26, 1985... I BETTER TAKE STOCK OF THE SITUATION...

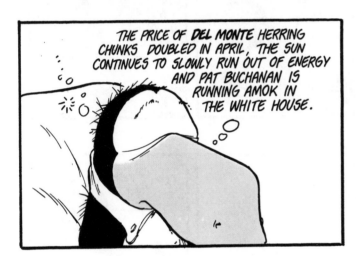

THE PRICE OF **DEL MONTE** HERRING CHUNKS DOUBLED IN APRIL, THE SUN CONTINUES TO SLOWLY RUN OUT OF ENERGY AND PAT BUCHANAN IS RUNNING AMOK IN THE WHITE HOUSE.

ON THE OTHER HAND, EATING DANDELIONS STILL HASN'T CAUSED CANCER IN RATS, SUMMER IS ONLY DAYS AWAY AND BROOKE SHIELDS HAS NOW SAFELY PASSED HER ACNE YEARS.

... ALL IN ALL, A REASONABLE AND STABLE BALANCE, METHINKS. PRESUMABLY, THE UNIVERSE CAN CARRY ON SMOOTHLY WITHOUT MY CONSCIOUS PRESENCE UNTIL AT LEAST... OH, LET'S SAY...

...NOON.

Z ZZ SNORT...
Z Z   Z ZZ

NOW.

144

SORRY...I'M IN NO MOOD TO DISCUSS APARTHEID, MR. JONES...

MY SISTER AND HER ENTIRE SORORITY JUST GOT ARRESTED AT THE UNIVERSITY FOR PROTESTING SOUTH AFRICA..AND I GOTTA GO BAIL THE LITTLE NITWIT OUT OF JAIL.

MARK MY WORDS...THIS 1985 BRAND OF COLLEGE RADICALISM IS GOING TO TEAR THE COUNTRY APART!!

I WON'T HUSH. THIS PLACE SMELLS LIKE AN ARMPIT AND I'M WRITING MRS. REAGAN ABOUT IT. WE'RE MISSING "ENTERTAINMENT TONIGHT". I KNOW IT...

HI, BIG BROTHER! WE'RE ON A 30-MINUTE HUNGER STRIKE! Y'ALL ARE ACTING LIKE A BUNCH OF GEEKS!

NO...WE'RE "GREEKS"...AND WE'RE STRIKING A BLOW FOR RACIAL HARMONY IN SOUTH AF-- KITZI, YOUR SORORITY DOESN'T EVEN ADMIT BLACKS!!

HOLD IT, GIRLS... CONTRADICTION CITY... I'M TELLIN' DAD ABOUT THIS!!

AND SO.. WITH SPRING IN THE AIR AND APARTHEID ON THE MIND, THE AMERICAN MEADOW PARTY CONVENED FOR A SPECIAL TÊTE-À-TÊTE ON SOUTH AFRICA...

IT'S... A MORAL... OUTRAGE!

BE SEATED

ONCE SETTLED...THE MEETING COMMENCED WITH EMOTIONS RUNNING HIGH...

BRING ON THE GUEST SPEAKER!

PLEASE WELCOME CHIEF DAN "BROKEN FEATHER", WHO'LL BE SPEAKING ON RACIAL SEGREGATION AND FORCED RESETTLEMENT THROUGHOUT AMERICAN HISTORY.

ZING!

OOPS! HOW TIME FLIES! GOTTA RUN! COLLECTIVE GUILT MAKES MY STOMACH ACHE...

SO I SAY ENOUGH DEMONSTRATIONS! ENOUGH ARRESTS! ENOUGH HUNGER STRIKES!

TODAY'S TOPIC: SOUTH AFRICA

IT IS TIME FOR MORE DIRECT ACTION! I HAVE A SECRET PLAN! BUT FOR SOME OF YOU OUT THERE, IT COULD MEAN ONLY ONE THING:

TODAY'S TOPIC: SOUTH AFRICA

...PERSONAL RISK.

TODAY'S TOPIC: SOUTH AFRICA

OOPS! IT'S GETTIN' LATE! I GOTTA DATE! "PERSONAL RISK" MAKES MY STOMACH ACHE!

145

NERVOUS. I'M NERVOUS. ASSIGNED TO GUARD OLIVER WHILE HE WORKS ON THIS SECRET ANTI-APARTHEID EXPERIMENT... I'M VERY, VERY NERVOUS...

ALL THIS RESEARCH COULD BE VERY UNETHICAL! OR ILLEGAL! OR WORSE... MORALLY SHAKY!

OPUS.. I'D LIKE YOU TO PICK UP A FEW INGREDIENTS FOR MY EXPERIMENTS..

OKAY. FINE, FINE.

THREE TABLESPOONS OF NEWT TONGUES...

I WILL NOT BE A PARTY TO THIS! NOPE! NOPE!

THE "ELECTRO-PHOTO PIGMENT-IZER" IS READY FOR TESTING.

YOUR UNSUSPECTING GUINEA PIG AWAITS AT THE TOP OF THE STAIRS, MR. EINSTEIN.

HELLO, STEVE. HOLD STILL AND CLOSE YOUR EYES.

WHAT'S THAT?

FLASH!

IT WORKS!

WHAT WORKS?

FLASH!

WELL! THAT IS A CLEVER DEVICE! NICE JOB, MR. JONES! WEARS OFF IN A FEW DAYS, DID YOU SAY?

APPARENTLY SO.

VERY STRIKING! WILL IT WORK ON ANYBODY? MEN? WOMEN? CHILDREN?...

... A SOUTH AFRICAN AMBASSADOR TO THE U.S.?

PERISH THE THOUGHT!

GREETINGS, STEVE! DID YOU HAPPEN TO SEE OLIVER GO --

FEELING YOURSELF TODAY, STEVE?

WHAT'S THAT MEAN? GIT OUTTA HERE.

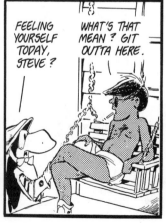

EXACTLY. I'LL GIT OUTTA HERE, GO HOME, LOCK THE DOOR, GET IN THE TUB AND SIMPLY PONDER THE WONDER OF IT ALL. THEN I'LL COME BACK OUT WHEN IT'S SAFE AGAIN.

HELLO STEVE! WHAT'S NEW?

I'M BLACK.

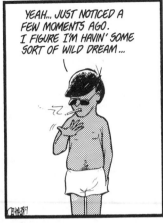

YEAH... JUST NOTICED A FEW MOMENTS AGO. I FIGURE I'M HAVIN' SOME SORT OF WILD DREAM...

ANY MOMENT NOW, I EXPECT ROD SERLING TO STROLL OUT FROM BEHIND A BUSH AND SAY, "FOR YOUR CONSIDERATION...MR. STEVE DALLAS, FORMERLY AN OCCASIONAL MUTTERER OF RACIAL SLURS... NOW AN 'EBONY' READER IN THE TWILIGHT ZONE."

OO! SOUNDS LIKE A GOOD EPISODE!

ROD?

FATHER?

YES?

MAY I HAVE PERMISSION TO SEND SOMEONE TO WASHINGTON, D.C., TO FLASH THE SOUTH AFRICAN AMBASSADOR WITH MY NEW "ELECTRO PHOTO PIGMENT-IZER", THEREBY TURNING HIM BLACK AND CREATING AN INTERNATIONAL DIPLOMATIC BROUHAHA?

YUPPIES RIOT

NO.

JUST THE USUAL FORMALITY BEFORE THE CHAOS BEGINS. LIKE PLAYING THE NATIONAL ANTHEM BEFORE A CUBS GAME.

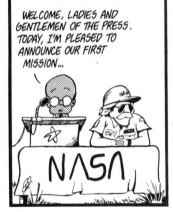

WELCOME, LADIES AND GENTLEMEN OF THE PRESS. TODAY, I'M PLEASED TO ANNOUNCE OUR FIRST MISSION...

NASA

CAPTAIN CUTTER JOHN, HERE, WILL MAKE A SUB-ORBITAL FLIGHT IN THE SHUTTLE CHAIR "ENTERPOOP," TO WASHINGTON, D.C., WHERE HE WILL FLASH THE SOUTH AFRICAN AMBASSADOR WITH MY "ELECTRO PHOTO PIGMENT-IZER."

NASA

YES, WE'RE ALL VERY EXCITED HERE AT NASA.

NASA

"NASA"?

"NATIONAL AIRBORNE SITTERS ASSOCIATION".

BY GOLLY, WE'VE GOT THE RUSSIANS BEAT THIS TIME!!

AND NOW...WE OF THE "NATIONAL AIRBORNE SITTERS ASSOCIATION" WOULD LIKE TO PRESENT THE SHUTTLE CHAIR "ENTERPOOP". OKAY... ROLL 'ER OUT!!

NASA

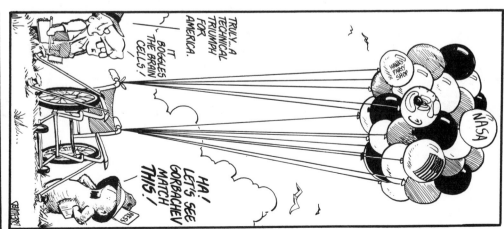

TRULY...A TECHNICAL TRIUMPH FOR AMERICA.

IT BOGGLES THE BRAIN CELLS!

HA! LET'S SEE GORBACHEV MATCH THIS!

HAWKS' PARTY SHOP

NASA

ZZZZ...
SNORE...
ZZZ...
SNORT!
ZZZ

ATTENTION YOUNG STUDENT BINKLEY! I AM *THE MASTER QUIZZER!* PREPARE YOURSELF FOR A POP QUIZ ON THE HOMEWORK YOU SHOULD HAVE BEEN DOING LAST NIGHT INSTEAD OF WATCHING TV!

BUT...BUT "DYNASTY" WAS ON!

NO TALKING! ANSWER THE FOLLOWING QUESTION CORRECTLY...IF NOT, YOUR FATHER WILL BE TURNED INTO AN *AVOCADO.*

AN AVOCADO!?

QUESTION: "IN WHAT YEAR DID CALVIN COOLIDGE MARRY HIS WIFE LORNA?"

UH... 1905?

WRONG! TRICK QUESTION! HER NAME WAS "GRACE"!

HMMPH!!

ACTUALLY, I ALWAYS KNEW SOMETHING LIKE THIS WAS GOING TO HAPPEN ONE DAY...

Oooo

SON... I'M VERY, *VERY* DISAPPOINTED IN YOU...

LAUNCH DAY! A FESTIVE MOOD IS IN THE AIR! THE SHIP IS PREPARED FOR BLAST-OFF...

SHUTTLE CHAIR LAUNCHING TODAY ABOUT 3 P.M.

MEANWHILE, SHUTTLE CHAIR ASTRONAUT CUTTER JOHN MENTALLY PREPARES HIMSELF FOR THE DANGEROUS VOYAGE AHEAD...

MMPH! MM! OO! SNORT! MMPH.

...WHILE THE ROYAL BLOOM COUNTY MARCHING BAND BELTS OUT A DOWNRIGHT ROUSING RENDITION OF "THE STARS AND STRIPES FOREVER"!

BOOM! BOOM! BOOM!

TIPS

...THE TUBA SECTION, HOWEVER, IS HAVING THE USUAL CONFUSION WITH THE SHEET MUSIC AND APPEARS TO BE WELL INTO THE THIRD VERSE OF MADONNA'S "LIKE A VIRGIN"...

BLATT! PHBLAT!

OOMP! PHOOP!

THE FINAL DANGEROUS TASK... LOADING THE MIGHTY SHUTTLE CHAIR'S MAIN BOOSTER FUEL...

PHSSSS...

HELIUM

HOLD IT. WHAT'S WRONG?

WE'VE RUN OUT.

HELIUM

AWRIGHT... WHO'S BEEN SUCKING ON THE HELIUM?!

I BET IT WAS SOMEONE IN THE BAND... YOU KNOW, MUSICIANS...

HELIUM

HEY... WHOA, IT WASN'T ME, MAN.

ME NEITHER!

SQUEAK!

LAUNCH '83

3..2..1... WE HAVE LIFT-OFF!!

UP UP AND AWAY IN MY BEEOOTIFUL BEEOOTIFUL WHEELCHAIR...

HOLD IT! THERE'S A BYSTANDER INTERFERING IN OPERATIONS!

YOW! I'M CAUGHT! HELP!! AAIGH! ASSISTANCE!

SIR! PLEASE REMOVE YOURSELF FROM THE LAUNCH SITE!

WHOA! HOLD ON! BE COOL! HOLD ON!

LAUNCH '83

WELL, WE APPEAR TO HAVE GAINED AN ASTRONAUT.

...AND LOST A THIRD-STRING TUBA PLAYER! MY GOD, PUT SOME VALUE ON THE MAN'S LIFE!!

CHICAGO, THIS IS TWA 649... WE'RE 70 MILES EAST OF VECTOR 12 WITH LITTLE WEATHER TO REPORT...

30 KNOT WINDS... CUMULUS CLOUDS AT 21,000 FEET... SLIGHT CHOPPINESS AT 24,000...

...AND A BIG-NOSED DWARF HANGING FROM A WHEELCHAIR AT 27,000.

I SAID, WHO'S DOWN THERE?

ED McMAHON. ARE WE ALMOST DOWN YET?

I'M SURE ALL OF YOU IN THE PRESS ARE CURIOUS ABOUT HOW THE SHUTTLE CHAIR MISSION IS GOING...

NASA

WELL, I'M HAPPY TO REPORT THAT IT'S ALL GOING VERY SMOOTHLY UP THERE! A-OKAY, ALL THE WAY!

NASA

EXCEPT, OF COURSE, FOR THE USUAL LITTLE PROBLEM WITH THE PLUMBING FACILITIES...

NASA

WHAT LITTLE PROBLEM?   WE DON'T HAVE ANY.

WELL THIS IS A FINE HOW-DO-YOU-DO!!

27,000 FEET UP IN THE AIR ON A WHEELCHAIR HEADING FOR WHO KNOWS WHERE, WITHOUT EVEN A FRESH CHANGE OF SKIVVIES ON HAND!

AND THE WORST... YES THE WORST INDIGNITY OF ALL... NO PLUMBING FACILITIES!!

NOT TO MENTION THIS IS THURSDAY AND I'LL BE MISSING "CHEERS".   HEY...WHOA... WE'RE NOT SAVAGES UP HERE...

OH, PARDON US, DEAR GENTLE COUNTRY PEOPLE...

PER CHANCE, COULD WE BEQUEST OF YOU TO TOSS UP A FEW APPLES, A HERRING BURGER AND A FRESH PAIR OF UNDERWEAR, SIZE EXTRA-SMALL?

GENTLE-MEN?   WANNA SHEWT 'EM?   YEP.

LADIES AND GENTLEMEN... CAPTAIN CUTTER JOHN HAS RADIOED IN AN EMERGENCY...

NASA

IT SEEMS THAT A FEW OF THE PROTECTIVE, HEAT-RESISTANT TILES WERE DAMAGED DURING THE LAUNCH...

NASA

HOWEVER, HE'S PLANNING A DARING ATTEMPT TO REPAIR THE DAMAGE BY DEPLOYING THE SHUTTLE CHAIR'S SPECIAL MECHANICAL ARM...

NASA

I DON'T SEE ANY STUPID TILES!   I KNOW! JUST KIDDIN'!

WE'RE GOING TO DIE, CUTTER JOHN... I *KNOW* IT! AND WHAT DREADFUL TIMING!

I'VE ALWAYS BELIEVED THAT YOU'LL END UP SPENDING ETERNITY WITH THE PERSON YOU'RE NEAREST TO WHEN YOU KICK THE BUCKET.

OKAY...SO I'M NOT GINA LOLLOBRIGIDA.

YOU *CERTAINLY* AREN'T.

WE'RE LOSING ALTITUDE! I HOPE THAT'S THE POTOMAC RIVER UNDER US!

IT'S THE ATLANTIC OCEAN... WE'RE ABOUT 1200 MILES OFF COURSE.

OH GREAT...OH GREAT... HOW'D I GET INTO THIS?! GIANT SQUIDS PROBABLY *LOVE* TO EAT SHORT, TUBBY TUBA PLAYERS!

QUICK! LIGHTEN THE LOAD! START FLAPPING!

NO GOOD! I'M FIGHTING 17 MILLION YEARS OF UNCOOPERATIVE AVIAN EVOLUTION!

MAYDAY! MAYDAY! MAYDAY!...

THE MISSION IS EXPERIENCING A FEW MINOR COMPLICATIONS...

DAY 7

NASA

C'MON, MR. NASA DIRECTOR... WHAT'S REALLY HAPPENING WITH THE SHUTTLE CHAIR?

NO COMMENT.

PRESS CAGE ←

PRESS

SOMETHING'S UP... NOW C'MON...OFF THE RECORD... I SWEAR ON MY HONOR AS A GRADUATE OF THE "RUPERT MURDOCH SCHOOL OF EXUBERANT JOURNALISM."

OFF THE RECORD?

OFF THE RECORD.

BINGO! The Bloom Beacon

SHUTTLE CHAIR "PILES IT IN" OVER ATLANTIC

MEDIOCRE TUBA PLAYER PRESUMED "DEAD AS A DOORKNOB"

SQUID BAIT?

FATHER.. I HAVE A CONFESSION TO MAKE.

LIFE

I WENT AGAINST YOUR WISHES AND LAUNCHED A SHUTTLE CHAIR TO WASHINGTON, D.C., TO FLASH THE SOUTH AFRICAN AMBASSADOR WITH MY "PIGMENT-IZER"...RESULTING IN THE PRESUMED DEATH OF CUTTER JOHN AND A LOCAL TUBA PLAYER.

LIFE

THANKS FOR BEING STRAIGHT WITH ME, SON. YOU'RE GROUNDED UNTIL YOUR 45TH BIRTHDAY.

LIFE

ACTUALLY, I WAS HOPING TO BE SENT TO BED WITHOUT ANY JELL-O.

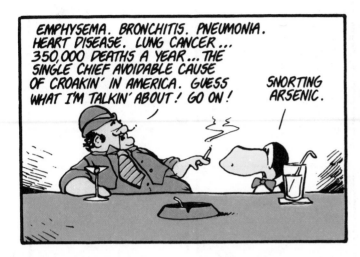

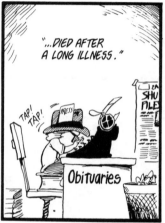

"...AND FINALLY, I, P. OPUS, DO BEQUEATH MY ENTIRE LIFE SAVINGS OF #64,397.34 TO..."

WHO?! WHO GETS ALL THE DOUGH?!

...TO THE INDIVIDUAL WHO HAS MOST ENRICHED MY LIFE WITH HIS LOVE AND SPIRITUAL LEADERSHIP...

AND WHO IS THAT?

ACKPH.

BILL!! BILL THE CAT! THIS IS BINKLEY! OPUS TRAGICALLY KICKED THE BUCKET AND LEFT YOU ALL HIS DOUGH!

YEAH! NO KIDDING! MILO IS HEADING OVER TO CHECK YOU OUT OF THE CLINIC TOMORROW! RIGHT!... YOU'RE COMIN' HOME!!

WHAT'S THAT?

CAN HE BRING HIS "GARFIELD" BEDPAN?

NO.

OH, GREAT AND HOLY ONE... I BESEECH YOU...

WHY, OH WHY DID THOU ALLOW THE BELOVED OPUS UNIT TO CROAK?!

SNIFF!

HE WAS SWEET AND SINCERE AND GIVING AND GOOD.. AND A CHERISHED NEIGHBOR UNDESERVING OF SUCH A FATE!!

NEVERTHELESS, BETTER HIM THAN ME. AMEN.

YA KNOW, DAD, OPUS' AND CUTTER JOHN'S DEATHS HAVE MADE ME REFLECT ON MY OWN MORTALITY... AND JUST HOW LITTLE TIME I HAVE LEFT.

DEPRESSING THOUGHTS, I CAN ASSURE YOU, UNTIL I CONSIDER OTHERS AROUND ME WHO, OF COURSE, HAVE DARN NEAR ONE FOOT IN THE GRAVE RIGHT NOW!

ME?

WELL, I MEAN, GOOD LORD... WHAT ARE YOU? 30?...32?

MR. MAESTRO! I... YOUR THIRD-STRING TUBA PLAYER, WILL NOT BE ATTENDING THE REHEARSAL TODAY!

REHEARSAL TODAY NO TARDINESS

I AM DEJECTED, DEPRESSED AND DEFINITELY IN DE DUMPS. SO TO SPEAK.

I AM STILL WITHOUT FEMALE COMFORT AND COMPANIONSHIP. WHY, I HAVEN'T INDULGED IN ANY SNUGGLEBUNNIES FOR AT LEAST... UH...WELL HECK, AT LEAST SINCE 1979. WELL, ACTUALLY NEVER. I WAS BORN IN '80.

ADMIT IT... A SHORT, BIG-NOSED, GOOFY-LOOKING FELLOW WHO LOOKS LIKE HE MIGHT SMELL LIKE AN OLD ANCHOVY PIZZA WILL JUST NEVER GET A HOT N' FANCY BABE .!!

BRUCE SPRINGSTEEN DID.

WHY, HE DID, DIDN'T HE?

YEP.

THANKS, BRUCE !

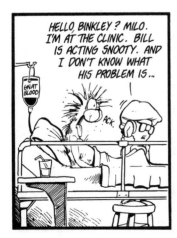

WELL... MILO IS ON HIS WAY BACK WITH BILL THE CAT.

APPARENTLY, HE'S TAKIN' THE BUS AGAIN.

I, MYSELF, DON'T MUCH CARE FOR BUSES.

ACK.

ACK YERSELF.

Dear Madam, I am sorry to inform you that your son, Opus, has fatally deceased recently.

He died trying to rescue American M.I.A.s in Vietnam while massacring hordes of subhuman communists, bloodthirsty Russians and cowardly U.S. bureaucrats, thereby single-handedly restoring America's greatness.

Regretfully Yours,
Milo Bloom

SOMEHOW, IT SOUNDED MORE FASHIONABLE THAN "EATEN BY SQUID."

I UNDERSTAND.

SOMEHOW, IT DIDN'T REALLY SINK IN BEFORE, MILO... I'VE BEEN FLOATING IN A SEA OF FALSE DENIAL...

BUT THIS... THIS BRINGS THE TERRIBLE REALITY HOME BRUTALLY...

POUND POUND POUND

I MEAN, MY GOSH.. OPUS IS REALLY GONE, ISN'T HE ?!

THE BLOOM BOARDING HOUSE
• NO WINOS
• NO WIMPS
• NO WALRUSES

WALRUSES WELCOME

SO! A FELLOW GETS A MODERATE INHERITANCE AND HIS VALUES GO OUT THE WINDOW, EH ?!

WHAT'S WRONG ?

LOOK WHAT I FOUND IN BILL'S ROOM !.. A WALL STREET JOURNAL ! A CENTERFOLD OF BOB DOLE FROM FORTUNE MAGAZINE ! AND A BROCHURE FOR A NEW CHRYSLER "LE BARON."

FIRST COCAINE... THEN CULTS... NOW REPUBLICANISM ! JUST A FOOL FOR THE LATEST PASSING FAD, AREN'T YOU ?!?

OH BINKLEY... HE'S SLIPPING AWAY FROM US AGAIN...

HEY... C'MON.. WE'LL BUY HIM AN OLD "VW" VAN...

I NEED TWO TICKETS TO NEW YORK CITY. GOT ANY SEATS LEFT IN THE CANCER SECTION?

SIR?

GATES 1-9

UNITED

YEAH?

YOUR TRAVELING COMPANION IS A LITTLE HESITANT ABOUT GOING THROUGH SECURITY.

UNITED

HEY! STOP CAUSIN' TROUBLE!! WHAT'D I TELL YOU ABOUT THIS? I SAID IT WON'T CAUSE STERILITY! ABSOLUTELY, POSITIVELY, NEARLY ALMOST NEVER EVER IN MOST CASES! NOW GET IN THERE! HEY!...

PLEASE LAY BAGS FLAT

ACK

X-RAY

OOF..

I DO BELIEVE I GOT ME A SHIITE MUSL'M HAHJACKER!

NO! NO! OFFICER...HE'S A PRESBYTERIAN.

AIRPORT SECURITY

GATE 29

PRESB'TERIAN? THEY HAHJACKERS?

NO... NONE SO FAR.

AIRPORT SECURITY

GATE 29

THEM GRENADES IN HIS MOUTH?

JUST SWOLLEN LYMPH NODES. TRUST ME.. HE'S GOT NO WEAPONS!

GATE 29

NONE 'CEPT HIS BREATH...COULD KILL A PIG AT FIFTY FEE—

WOOSH!

GATE 29

THEY MUST BE ABOUT READY TO TAPE THE SHOW OVER IN NEW YORK, RIGHT ALONG NOW...

YA KNOW, STEVE IS HOPING THIS INTERVIEW WILL SNARE A FEW MOVIE OFFERS FOR BILL...HE'S VERY EXCITED!

ONE WOULD HOPE, HOWEVER, THAT STEVE HAS ACTUALLY SEEN THE LETTERMAN SHOW BEFORE..

ONE WOULD HOPE..

..AND THEN AFTER THE TERI GARR SEGMENT, YOU TWO COME OUT FOR "STUPID PET TRICKS"...

ACK

STUPID WHAT?

GREEN ROOM

THE DAVID LETTERMAN SHOW

MILO! THIS IS STEVE! I'M BACKSTAGE AT THE LETTERMAN SHOW...THEY'VE GOT US IN A ROOM FILLED WITH INSANE PEOPLE AND THEIR WEIRD PETS!

..JUST WHAT KIND OF TALK-SHOW IS THIS, ANYWAY?!

EXCUSE ME.. MY PYTHON "HUGGY" IS GIVING YOUR CAT'S FOOT A LOVE HUG.

MY GOD... LOOKIT THIS!! A SNAKE IS SWALLOWING BILL'S LEG!!

HE LOVES TO GIVE HUGS.. THAT'S WHY WE CALL HIM "HUGGY"!

DOES THIS HAPPEN ON "MERV"?!

NOW "HUGGY" IS HUGGING HIS HEAD!

AND NOW.. WAKE THE KIDS, CALL THE NEIGHBORS... IT'S TIME FOR "STUPID PET TRICKS." FIRST UP IS MR. STEVE DALLAS AND HIS CAT, BILL.

LOOK, LETTERMAN..WE CAME TO DO AN INTERVIEW. BILL, HERE, IS A FILM STAR AND A RECENTLY RE-FORMED COKE FIEND.. NOW-- HAVE HIM DO A TRICK!

A TRICK? YOU WANT A TRICK? FINE... HERE'S A ☆∂#✳?! TRICK...

BILL, GO THROW UP A HAIR BALL ON PAUL SHAFFER.

WHOOP! THAT'S IT FOR TONIGHT, FOLKS! GOODNIGHT! DRIVE SAFELY!

BILL! IT'S 5 A.M.! WHERE'VE YA BEEN?! HEY... ARE YOU GETTING MIXED UP WITH A WOMAN?! WHO?! WHO IS IT?!

WHAT'S THIS? TODAY'S "NEW YORK POST?"

NEW YORK POST JULY

AROUND TOWN

FUN COUPLE
Jeane Kirkpatrick and Friend
5th Ave. Pizza Hut for
drinks and a
giggli...

SHE'S TROUBLE, BILL.. T-R-O-U-B-L-E !!

THPT.

THAT WAS THE BELL HOP. THERE'S A PACKAGE FOR YOU.

IT'S A BOX OF CHOCOLATES IN THE SHAPE OF NICARAGUA.

"FOR MY BILL, LET'S DEVOUR IT TOGETHER. HUNGRILY, JEANE KIRKPATRICK."

WHY DOES THIS ALL MAKE ME ITCH?

BILL...YOU CAN'T BE SEEN WITH KIRKPATRICK AGAIN...SOMEONE MIGHT NOTICE..HOLLYWOOD IS STILL VERY LIBERAL.. OKAY? BILL?

WHIRRR...

HEY.. SHE EATS LEFTISTS FOR BREAKFAST!! WHAT IF WARREN BEATTY COMES OVER WITH A SCRIPT?!...

KNOCK! KNOCK!

OH..HELLO, MADAM AMBASSADOR. YES..HE'LL BE OUT IN A MINUTE. WOULD YOU MIND HIDING BEHIND THAT PALM WHILE YOU WAIT? THANK YOU.

THERE'S STILL TIME! WHAT ABOUT BETTY FRIEDAN?..

THPTH.

165

HELLO.. THIS IS THE NEW YORK CITY POLICE.. YEAH?

WE'RE HOLDING A ONE MISTER BILL THE CAT.

WHAT'D HE DO?

HE WAS SEEN WITH AN UNIDENTIFIED WOMAN IN MANHATTAN LAST NIGHT SPRAY PAINTING THE WALLS OF THE RUSSIAN TEA ROOM WITH "GORBACHEV IS A WEENIE!"

KNOW HIM?

NOT EVEN VAGUELY. GOOD NIGHT.

HOLD ME, KISS ME, SQUEEZE ME, RUB ME... BABY, LAY THOSE LIPS UPON ME.

PERSONAL COMPUTERS ARE CAPABLE OF SUCCUMBING TO A MOMENTARY IMPULSE OF WILD ABANDON!!

IT WAS A DARK AND STORMY NIGHT...
A HUDDLED, SHIVERING FIGURE MOVES ACROSS THE HORIZON TOWARD THE BLOOM COUNTY BOARDING HOUSE...

HE WALKS WEARILY.. HEAVILY... AS IF EXHAUSTED FROM A LONG JOURNEY.. AS IF SQUID HAD BEEN NIBBLING HIS TOES RECENTLY...

BUT WITH HIM COME OUR QUESTIONS... WHERE IS HE FROM? WHAT DOES HE WANT?... AND, FOR CRYING OUT LOUD...

".. JUST WHO IS THIS DARK, WET MYSTERY FIGURE?!"

CLUE

·SIGH··

BANG! BANG! BANG!

OKAY OKAY OKAY... I'M COMING..

GREAT JUMPIN' JACK RABBITS.

GOOD EVENING. I DON'T KNOW WHERE I CAME FROM AND I CAN'T REMEMBER WHO I AM... I DO, HOWEVER, KNOW THAT I AM ABOUT TO PASS OUT RIGHT ON MY HONKER.

PART OF ME WANTS TO SCREAM WITH JOY AND THE OTHER PART WANTS TO SET HIM OUT WITH THE TRASH AND GO BACK TO BED IN BLISSFUL IGNORANCE.

LISTEN...WE NEED TO TALK. YOU'RE SIMPLY NOT...A MAN.

ARE YOU CALLING ME A WIMP?

NO NO...I'M CALLING YOU A...WELL...HOW SHOULD I PUT THIS...?

OPUS, YOU'RE AN Aptenodytes patagonica.

BEG PARDON?

YOU'RE A PENGUIN.

AND YOU'RE AN AMOEBA! HOW DO YOU DO?

LOOK...IT'S NEVER EASY TO SUDDENLY COME FACE-TO-FACE WITH THE BRUTAL REALITY OF ONESELF.

A PENGUIN? I'M A... PENGUIN?

WHAT'S WRONG WITH A PENGUIN?

I DUNNO... THEY'RE SO... RIDICULOUS.

ARE YOU SURE?...ARE YOU POSITIVELY SURE I'M NOT REALLY SOMETHING ELSE?!

LOOK AT YOURSELF... WHAT ELSE?

A REFUGEE FROM A SHRINERS' PARADE? GOSH...I DUNNO..

THEY SAY I'M A PENGUIN, EH? THIS? THIS IS A PENGUIN?...

..A ROTUND BELLY..A SWAY BACK..FLAT, DAMP FEET... A MORE-THAN-GENEROUS HONKER..A TAD LOPSIDED AND SLIGHTLY MUSHY TO THE TOUCH...

AND A SIZABLE, WELL-CUSHIONED TUSH...LUMPY AND MELLOW WITH AGE...LIKE A FINE CHEESE. YESSIR... WHATEVER I AM OR AM NOT, ONE THING REMAINS CERTAIN...

..., I'M ALMOST STARTLINGLY GOOD LOOKING.

WHERE'S "MR. AMNESIA?"

GONE.

HE'S OUT THERE SOMEWHERE FINDING HIMSELF...REDISCOVERING EXACTLY WHO HE IS... WHAT HE IS...

YES..HE'S A BLANK SLATE OUT ON A FRIGHTENING JOURNEY OF SELF-DISCOVERY!!

"...FEATHERED BUT FLIGHTLESS, THESE CHEERFUL CLOWNS-OF-THE-ICE FROLIC IN THE SOUTH ATLANTIC, FEEDING ON HERRING, SMALL COD AND HOSTESS `DING-DONGS'..."

169

RRING6! RRING6!

HELLO. YOU HAVE REACHED THE ESTATE OF LUTHER HENRY PUTTGRASS AND WIFE. THE FORMER IS SPEAKING.

THIS IS AN ABC NEWS / WASHINGTON POST POLL... ARE YOU OR ARE YOU NOT IN FAVOR OF SPACE-BASED WEAPON RESEARCH AND THE PRESIDENT'S STRATEGIC DEFENSE INITIATIVE?

AM I OR AM I NOT IN FAVOR OF SPACE-BASED WEAPON RESEARCH AND THE STRATEGIC DEFENSE INITIATIVE?

LOUELLA! THERE IS AN INQUIRY INTO THE STATUS OF MY CURRENT POSITION ON SPACE-BASED WEAPON RESEARCH AND THE STRATEGIC DEFENSE INITIATIVE.

THANK GOD I'M IN A COUNTRY WHICH SEEKS THE VIEWS OF SOMEONE LIKE ME, LUTHER HENRY PUTTGRASS, CITIZEN AND TV REPAIRMAN... LITTLE FISH AMONG TROUT... MINOR SPOKE IN THE GREAT WHEEL OF LIFE...INSIGNIFI— CANT BLOB OF SPITTLE IN IN THE GREAT UNIVERSAL CESSPOOL. LOUELLA! TELL HIM JUST EXACTLY WHAT I'M IN FAVOR OF...

MORE SKIN ON "LOVE BOAT".

AND FOR FURTHER CONTEMPLATION ON MATTERS OF NATIONAL POLICY, L.H. PUTTGRASS HEADS FOR THE TUB. ALERT TED KOPPEL.

"A PENGUIN'S DAILY ROUTINE WILL INCLUDE MANY LONG, HOT SHOWERS AND THE SENSUAL BLOW-DRYING OF THEIR PLUMAGE, FOLLOWED BY COUNTLESS LEISURE HOURS SPENT PERUSING BACK ISSUES OF 'HARPER'S' AND 'TV GUIDE'..."

HMM...

"...AND THEN A MEAL OF COLD, JELLIED HERRING ENTRAILS WITH CATSUP."

OH GIVE ME A BREAK...

"COURTSHIP BEHAVIOR OF THE COMMON PENGUIN BEGINS WITH THE MALE QUICKLY BUT GENTLY MAKING A GRAB FOR THE FEMALE'S SHINS... AN IRRESISTIBLE OBJECT TO THE MALE PENGUIN..."

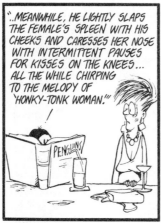

"...MEANWHILE, HE LIGHTLY SLAPS THE FEMALE'S SPLEEN WITH HIS CHEEKS AND CARESSES HER NOSE WITH INTERMITTENT PAUSES FOR KISSES ON THE KNEES... ALL THE WHILE CHIRPING TO THE MELODY OF 'HONKY-TONK WOMAN.'"

HEL-LO HOT MAMA!

WOOSH!

TIME FOR THE EVENING NEWS! AND THE QUESTION IS, SHALL I GO FOR THE GRAY-SPECKLED MATURITY OF THE INTENSE YET DAPPER DAN RATHER..?

..OR INSTEAD, THE QUIET CONFIDENCE AND SEXY INTELLIGENCE OF THE ETERNALLY ELOQUENT, HOPELESSLY HONEY-TONGUED PETER JENNINGS..?

.. OR RATHER STILL, THE BOYISH AND PLUCKY "TWINKLE-IN-THE-EYE" CHARM OF THE EVER YOUTHFUL...EVER PLAYFUL TOM BROKAW?

WHICH, OH WHICH SHALL IT BE?

JUMPIN' JEHOSAPHAT! WHO IS THIS TERRIBLE FELLOW?

BILL THE NEWLY WEALTHY CAT...

..WHO IS, EVEN AS WE SPEAK, TOOLING AROUND NEW YORK WITH JEANE KIRKPATRICK IN YOUR '39 CADILLAC ZEPHYR AND SPENDING YOUR LIFE SAVINGS... ALL OF WHICH YOU LEFT HIM IN YOUR WILL.

I DIDN'T.

YOU DID.

APPARENTLY I'M A BIT OF A YOGURT-HEAD.

IT HAS BEEN REMARKED.

WHO AM I? WHAT AM I ALL ABOUT? THIS AMNESIA IS THE PITS! I FEEL LIKE AN UNFINISHED PAINTING...

DO I PREFER SPINACH SALADS FOR LUNCH?...OR PISTACHIO-NUT ICE CREAM? DO I READ SAUL BELLOW?... OR STEPHEN KING?

AND FOR GOODNESS SAKE, DO I HAVE GOOD TASTE IN PERSONAL ATTIRE?... OR DEPLORABLE TASTE?

SLOWLY, THE TRUTH REARS ITS UGLY HEAD...

OPUS, WE'RE GIVING YOU YOUR OLD JOB BACK.

MY JOB? I DON'T REMEMBER... WHAT JOB?

THE ONE HERE AT THE "BLOOM BEACON."

REALLY! A JOURNALIST! MY! PROTECTOR OF THE PEOPLE! DEFENDER OF THE UNION!

RIGHT. AND THERE'S YOUR DESK.

WHERE? WHERE?

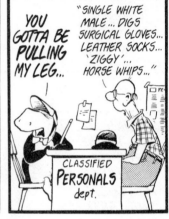

YOU GOTTA BE PULLING MY LEG...

"SINGLE WHITE MALE... DIGS SURGICAL GLOVES... LEATHER SOCKS... 'ZIGGY'... HORSE WHIPS..."

YES, MISTER "PERSONALS" EDITOR?

MY AMNESIA IS MAKING THIS JOB DIFFICULT. WHAT, EXACTLY, ARE MY MORALS?

I MEAN, AM I EASILY OUTRAGED BY IMMORAL LANGUAGE, PRURIENT TENDENCIES AND SHAMEFULLY ADULTEROUS DESIRES?

YEP. THAT'S YOU.

I SEE. THANK YOU.

YOU'RE WELCOME.

SHAME, SHAME, MRS. PIDDLBY!

"TO MY CONSTITUENTS: I, SENATOR LOU PHIPPS, ENJOY DRESSING UP LIKE JOAN COLLINS EVERY CHANCE I GET..."

"I...I ALSO LIVE FOR RUNNING UP AND DOWN MY SIDEWALK AT 4 a.m. WEARING ONLY A PAIR OF MAGIC RUBY SLIPPERS AND YELLING 'TOTO! TOTO!'"

IS THAT "TOTO" WITH TWO "T"S OR--

HONESTY... A RARE TRAIT IN A PUBLIC OFFICIAL, DON'T YOU THINK?

173

GOOD MORNING.

GOOD MORNING.

PERSONALS dept.

"SINGLE, WHI—"

I QUIT!!

CLICK...
TAP! TAP!

BOOP!
TAP.
TAP. BEEP...

BEEP...
CLICK.. CLICK...
BOOP!

"WELCOME, COMRADE, TO THE MAIN WORD-PROCESSING COMPUTER FOR THE GLORIOUS DAILY NEWSPAPER OF THE SOVIET SOCIALIST REPUBLICS: 'PRAVDA'."

TINGLING WITH EXCITEMENT, THE JUNIOR HACKER PAUSES TO CATCH WIND IN FERVENT ANTI-CIPATION OF THROWING THE FLAGSHIP OF COMMUNIST JOURNALISM INTO A GLORIOUS STATE OF UTTER HIGGLEDY-PIGGLEDY.

TODAY'S "PRAVDA," FRESH FROM THE LIBRARY! COMPLETE WITH CUSTOM HEADLINE...

WHAT'S IT SAY?

EXACTLY WHAT WE WROTE... "GORBACHEV URGES DISARMAMENT: TOTAL! UNILATERAL!"

YOU SURE ABOUT THE TRANSLATION?

SURE I'M SURE. I'M PRETTY SURE...

"GORBACHEV SINGS TRACTORS: TURNIP! BUTTOCKS!"

TODAY THE WORLD IS STILL REELING FROM YESTERDAY'S MYSTERIOUS HEADLINE IN "PRAVDA."...

IT READ, "GORBACHEV SINGS TRACTORS: TURNIP! BUTTOCKS!" THE DEFENSE DEPT. WOULDN'T COMMENT. HOWEVER, SECRETARY WEINBERGER LOOKED NOTICEABLY SHAKEN ALL DAY.

SO, AS NATO AND WARSAW PACT TROOPS REMAIN ON HIGH ALERT, MILLIONS ARE ASKING, WHAT DOES IT MEAN? AND WHO IS BEHIND IT?

WHO! INDEED, WHO!

THE GUESS IS MR. OLIVER WENDELL JONES OF 667 WEST MAPLE STREET. THE F.B.I. IS HEADING THERE RIGHT NOW.

175

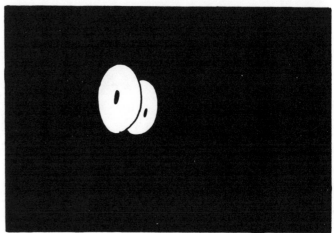

WHO ARE YOU?

I-I-I-I'M FROM THE STATE DEPARTMENT... W-W-WOULD MISTER TERRORIST LIKE TO NEGOTIATE?

HE'LL ONLY TALK TO THE TOP BANANA... THE "AUTHORITY ELITE".

OKAY! I'LL G-G-GET THE PRESIDENT! IS THAT WHO HE WANTS ME TO GET? ASK HIM! ASK HIM!

BRYANT GUMBEL.

DO I LOOK LIKE I HAVE THAT SORT OF CLOUT?!

LISTEN UP, MISTER NETWORK PRES... I WANT ONE FULL HOUR OF PRIME-TIME COVERAGE... OR THE CAT AND THE LAWYER DIE.

WE'LL GIVE YOU TWO HOURS.

TWO?

OKAY, MAKE IT THREE.

THREE?

AWRIGHT... TWIST MY ARM, YOU MURDEROUS THUG... MAKE IT FOUR HOURS!

I DON'T WANT FOUR!

FIVE! FIVE AND A SPECIAL BULLETIN DURING "COSBY"; YOU ANIMAL!!

A HOSTAGE CRISIS! MY NEWS INSTINCTS ARE TINGLING... I...I MUST RESTRAIN MYSELF...

"...I WILL NOT EXPLOIT THE HOSTAGES! I WILL NOT COVER THE STORY BY MERGING WITH IT! I...I WILL NOT RUN AMOK IN RABID, COMPETITIVE EXCESS...

"I....I..."

OH YES I WILL!! I WILL, OH GOD, I WILL!!

OPUS! YER OFF THE "PERSONALS" DESK AND YER ON THE HOSTAGE STORY!

GO INTERVIEW AND STAND VIGIL OVER ONE OF BILL THE CAT'S FAMILY MEMBERS OR CLOSEST FRIENDS.

BUT I'M HIS CLOSEST FRIEND.

THEN REPORT ON YOURSELF! BUT I WANT THAT "PERSONAL GRIEF" ANGLE!!

OKAY! OKAY!

PARDON ME. MAY I COME IN AND HANG AROUND YOUR LIVING ROOM FOR THE NEXT SEVERAL WEEKS?

NO! GO AWAY, YOU VULTURES!

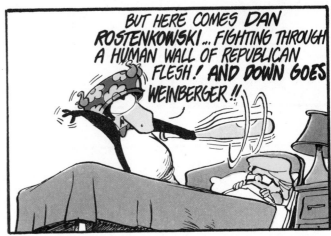

182

TONIGHT'S BIG STORY:
POLICE PREDICT "THE SHOWER
MARAUDER" COULD STRIKE
AGAIN AT ALMOST
ANY MOMENT...

REPORTS INDICATE HE'LL
PROBABLY SNEAK INTO A LOCAL
HOME WHERE A TV IS ON AND
THE OCCUPANT IS TAKING A
LONG HOT SHOWER...

THE INTENDED VICTIM, PROBABLY
SHORT, FAT AND WEARING A FLOWERED
SHOWER CAP, WILL NEVER HEAR HIS
ATTACKER ENTER THE BATHROOM
AND HIDE BEHIND
THE DOOR...

SLOWLY... SILENTLY.. THE KILLER WILL
SNEAK TOWARD THE SHOWER... HE
GRINS INSANELY.. THE AXE IS RAISED...
HIGHER... HIGHER... THE VICTIM STOPS...
LISTENS FOR THE TV...
AND THEN...

..AND THEN
WHAT?! WHAT?
WHAT? WHAT?

—THE VICTIM YELLS
WITH HYSTERICAL
PARANOIA...SHAKING
HIS LITTLE
SCRUBBER...

THE OUTDOORS! THE TOTAL NATURE EXPERIENCE! I LOVE IT!

MILO'S MEADOW

TAKE HEED, OH SINGULAR REMAINING DANDELION... I'M A-COMIN' TO JUMP ON YA!!

UH, OH.

NO RUNNIN'. NO JUMPIN'. NO PICKIN'. NO SPITTIN'. NO GRABBIN'. NO YELLIN'. NO SKINNY DIPPIN'...PUBLIC TOILETS ARE A DIME AND HAVE A NICE DAY.

ENTERING DANDELION NATIONAL PARK

DON'T TOUCH

WELCOME TO DANDELION NATIONAL PARK. THERE'Z TRAILER HOOK-UPS STILL AVAILABLE AT CAMPGROUND #74.

ENTERING DANDELION NATIONAL PARK

DON'T TOUCH

AERIAL TRAMWA

YES..WELL, WHAT I'D LIKE IS TO —–

'SCUSE ME FOR A SECOND, SON.

ENTERING DANDELION NATIONAL PARK

DON'T TOUCH

AERIAL TRAMWAY

LADY! YA CAN'T PARK YER TWO-TON "R.V." BY THE SNACK BAR...AND GIT YER LITTLE ONE TO STOP PIDDLIN' ON THE BEARS... MAKES 'EM GRUMPY!!

AS I WAS SAYING... I'D LIKE TO JUMP ON A DANDELION.

JUMP ON A–? SON, YOU EVER HEARD OF MAINTAININ' THE NATURAL BALANCE OF THINGS?

ENTERING DANDELION NATIONAL PARK

DON'T TOUCH

AERIAL TRAMW

GOIN' OUT, SON?

I'M ON "COMET ALERT."

SO SOON?

ONE SIMPLY DOES NOT RISK MISSING THE SINGLE MOST SPECTACULAR COMET FLIGHT IN MODERN CELESTIAL HISTORY. I AM LIVING JUST FOR THAT MAGIC MOMENT.

WHOOP! THERE IT WENT!

WHAT?! WHERE??

JOKE, SON.

DON'T DO THAT!!

LONELY AND SHIVERING... THE FAMED ASTRONOMER KEEPS A MIDNIGHT VIGIL FOR "THE COMET..."

..SCANNING THE VAST, SAVAGE REACHES OF THE COSMIC VOID, HIS MIND WANDERS TO THE FANTASTIC...TO THE UNFATHOM- ABLE...COULD HE BE STARING INTO THE VERY FACE OF...OF GOD HIMSELF?

BLEAH!

NO... I CERTAINLY DO NOT THINK THAT CARL SAGAN WOULD HAVE HANDLED THAT SITUATION WITH MORE POISE...

YOU'VE HEARD, OF COURSE, THAT OLIVER WENDELL JONES IS PREDICTING HALLEY'S COMET WILL STRIKE THE EARTH..
YOU JEST!

IT'S TRUE. WE'RE DOOMED.
SURELY YOU JEST!

THERE'S NOTHING WE CAN DO.
BUT OF COURSE THERE IS!

PENALTIES, SHMENALTIES... I'M CASHING IN MY I.R.A.!

"ALTHOUGH LITTLE PANIC HAS SURFACED AMONG THE LOCAL POPULACE, THERE HAS BEEN NOTICED A SUBTLE SENSE OF...
COMET TO RAM EARTH IN SIX MONTHS
Personals Editor

...GENERAL URGENCY ABOUT THINGS."
HURRY.. GET THIS DOWN: "WOMAN SEEKS MATE. QUICK."
Personals Dept.

TALL? SHORT? FAT?...
ANYBODY. WHO'S THAT?
Personals Dept.

THE JANITOR.
I'LL TAKE 'IM.
Personals Dept.

SIX MONTHS...THAT'S ALL ME AND THIS WORLD HAVE LEFT. SIX MONTHS TO LIVE A LIFETIME... AND SO MUCH LEFT TO DO!
TAKE 'ER EASY, OPUS BUDDY.

MADAM.. SURELY YOU WOULDN'T HAVE A POOR, YOUNG BOY FACE DEATH WITHOUT FIRST TASTING THE SWEET, FORBIDDEN FRUIT OF A WOMAN'S LOVE?
NOW WAIT JUST—

SMACK! SMACK! SMACK! SMACK! SMACK! SMACK!

YOU CAN TAKE ME NOW, COMET BABY... MY CUP DONE RUNNETH OVER!
EXCUSE HIM..HE'S HAD TOO MANY "SHIRLEY TEMPLE COCKTAILS".

WE'RE DOOMED! YES, DOOMED BY A COMET! WE'LL ALL BE BLOWN TO SMITHEREENS!!

SO...SO LITTLE TIME LEFT! FROM HERE ON I WANT MEALS OF ICE CREAM! ENDLESS BUBBLE BATHS! GOBS OF LOOSE WOMEN FEEDING ME PEELED GRAPES...
COME ALONG. LET'S GET YOU SOME HELP.

"H-HELP"? NO, NO... YOU DON'T MEAN...
THAT'S RIGHT.

ADVICE 5¢ DR. LUCY VAN PELT
THE DOCTOR IS
NOT SEEING ANY STUPID WATERFOWL

190

THE MANAGEMENT OF THIS FEATURE, IN CONJUNCTION WITH "BIG PIG PEACHES", PRESENTS THE FOLLOWING AEROBICS INSTRUCTION FOR THE PUBLIC'S BENEFIT.

A HEALTHY AND FIT COMICS READER IS A LAUGHING AND JOYOUS COMICS READER.

SOME MAY WISH TO CONSULT A PHYSICIAN BEFORE ATTEMPTING THESE EXERCISES.

OKEY-DOKE ... "LEFT FOREARM BENDS"... HUP! HUP! HUP! HUP!

"EAR-WIGGLING"! HUP! HUP! HUP! HUP! ONE MORE ... HUP!

WIGGLE WIGGLE   WIGGLE

THANK YOU FOR JOINING ALONG! PEACHES HAS SCHEDULED THE NEXT WORKOUT FOR TUESDAY, APRIL 9, 2014. SEE YOU THEN!

OH LORD, HAVE MERCY...

DUE TO NUMEROUS COMPLAINTS REGARDING THE LACK OF HELPFUL AEROBIC INFORMATION IN YESTERDAY'S INSTALLMENT, WE NOW CONTINUE WITH FURTHER VALUABLE EXERCISE TIPS ...

ALL OF US HERE AT BLOOM COUNTY REALLY CARE ABOUT YOUR BODY. TRULY. YOU HAVE NO IDEA.

PROFESSIONAL COACHING IS ALWAYS A PLUS IN SERIOUS AEROBICS.

GO GO GO GO GO GO GO GO GO GO GO GO GO GO GO GO GO GO GO GO ...   OOF! OOF! OOF! OOF!

COACH PEACHES

LONG RESTS BETWEEN EXERCISES ARE NOT CONDUCIVE TO HEALTHY CARDIO-VASCUBULAR WHATEVER.

WAKE UP! JUMPING JACKS! GET GOIN'! HEY!

COACH PEACHES   ZZZ...

GOOD DISCIPLINE IS ALWAYS A MUST FOR PROPER AEROBICS INSTRUCTION. LAZINESS IS A NO-NO!

I SAID GET GOIN' BLUBBER BUTT!

WAP! WAP! WAP! WAP! WAP! WAP!

A GOOD WAY TO WIND UP YOUR 370 MINUTES OF SPECIAL BLOOM COUNTY AEROBICS IS TO SPEND AN HOUR OR TWO PUMPING A LITTLE IRON ...

C'MON! LET'S GET PHYSICAL, FLABBY COMICS READERS!

...IF WEIGHTS AREN'T AVAILABLE, ALMOST ANYTHING HEFTY WILL SUFFICE!

OH, YOU ARE **NOT** SERIOUS...

COACH PEACHES

AT THE SAME TIME, WORK OFF THAT POST-AEROBIC TENSION WITH A JAUNTY, BRISK WALK!

FASTER! PICK IT UP! PUT THE PEDAL TO THE METAL!

GRUNT! OOF! OOF!   COACH PEACHES

AND THEN REWARD YOURSELF WITH A CUCUMBER SALAD AND AVOCADO YOGURT...YOU DESERVE IT, MR. HEALTHY!

ONE "BOO-BOO" BURGER...HEAVY GREASE!

OOF...   BOO BURG

NO MORE KINKY SECRETARIES! NO MORE LONELY STOCK-BROKERS! THIS BOY HAS BEEN PROMOTED!

LA MM MM...   PERSONAL

Personals DESK

NO UNFASHIONABLE SEXUAL METAPHORS PLEASE

PHOOEY WITH "PERSONALS"! ONWARD AND UPWARD TO A LITTLE SERIOUS JOURNALISM!

SERIOUS JOURNALISTS →

GOODNESS KNOWS, I'VE HAD JUST ABOUT **ENOUGH** OF THOSE GOOFY, WHITE, UPPER-MIDDLE-CLASS URBAN TYPES...

LIFESTYLES EATING BRIE WHILE WATCHING "CHEERS": A NEW TREND?

Lifestyles SECTION

A NEW NOSE! I FEEL GREAT! RENEWED! REBORN!

HEY, SIZZLIN' MAMA, COME ON OVER HERE AND LET THIS LOVE-GLADIATOR DANCE IN YOUR FIRES.

MORE SELF-CONFIDENT, TOO!

PORTNOY... DID YOU HEAR THE LATEST?

NO. WHAT?

--WE INTERRUPT THIS FEATURE TO EXPLAIN THE VARIOUS OBJECTS WHICH SEVERAL READERS HAVE NOTICED CLEVERLY OBSCURING THE SURGICALLY ALTERED NOSE OF ONE OF THE PRINCIPAL CHARACTERS...

THE U.S. SENATE HAS DETERMINED THAT THE GRAPHIC DEPICTION OF RADICAL COSMETIC BODY SURGERY, LIKE OBSCENE ROCK MUSIC, CAN POLLUTE THE MINDS OF YOUNG PEOPLE AND LEAD TO WIDESPREAD HEDONISM AND SECULAR HUMANISM. THUS, THE SELF-CENSORSHIP.

WE NOW RETURN TO TO THE HILARIOUS COMIC ALREADY IN PROGRESS...

TURNIPS! TURNIPS AND ANTIFREEZE!

NOT WITH DONNY OSMOND HE WON'T!!

♪ HMMM.. HMM.. ♪

...WE AGAIN INTERRUPT THIS FEATURE TO ANNOUNCE THAT, STARTING IMMEDIATELY, THERE WILL NO LONGER BE ANY EFFORT TO CONCEAL THE RESULTS OF THE PRINCIPAL CHARACTER'S RECENT NOSE JOB WITH VARIOUS CAREFULLY PLACED OBJECTS.

THIS COMIC WILL NO LONGER SUCCUMB TO THE DEMANDS OF THE PARENTAL-ACTION GROUPS WHICH SEEK TO PROTECT AMERICA'S YOUTH FROM VIEWING THIS INCREASINGLY COMMON FORM OF SHOCKING PERSONAL EXPRESSION.

LIFE...IS NOT ALWAYS PRETTY.

WE NOW RETURN TO THE UNCENSORED PANEL ALREADY IN PROGRESS...

♪ HMMM HMM...

A BLOOM COUNTY TELEPHONE POLL

THE MANAGEMENT OF THIS FEATURE WOULD LIKE TO SOLICIT THE OPINIONS OF YOU, THE VIEWERS, ON A SUBJECT OF SUDDEN AND UNEXPECTED IMPORTANCE... OPUS' NOSE.

WHY IS IT ANY OF THEIR BUSINESS?

BETWEEN NOW AND 7:15 P.M. TONIGHT, PLEASE DIAL: 1-800-555-6001 IF YOU PREFER THE NEW, IMPROVED NOSE. 1-800-555-6002 IF YOU PREFER THE OLD, "CLASSIC" NOSE. OR 1-800-555-6003 IF YOU THINK TV EVANGELIST PAT ROBERTSON, WITH OR WITHOUT A NOSE, SHOULD TEAM UP WITH BHAGWAN SHREE RAJNEESH AND FORM A REPUBLICAN "DREAM TICKET" IN 1988.

WHEN YOU REACH OUR SWITCHBOARD, YOUR VOTE WILL BE INSTANTLY REGISTERED.. AT WHICH TIME MRS. GRABOWSKI HERE WILL IMMEDIATELY SAY, "SORRY, YOUR CALL CAN NOT BE COMPLETED...", WHICH FOOLS THE PHONE CO. INTO NOT CHARGING US FOR THE CALL.

OFFICIAL SWITCHBOARD

TOMORROW WE'LL RELEASE THE RESULTS.

WHY DO I HAVE THE FEELING THAT DEMOCRACY AND "HONKER AESTHETICS" MAKE AN EXPLOSIVE COMBINATION?

THE NATIONAL PHONE-IN POLL REGARDING OPUS' NEW NOSE IS OVER. LET'S GO TO THE COMPUTER ROOM FOR THE RESULTS...

I HAVE **TOTAL** FAITH IN THE INTELLIGENCE AND COMMON "HORSE SENSE" OF THE NOBLE MASSES...

AHEM. THE RESULTS ✱ ARE AS FOLLOWS...

✱ THE MARGIN OF ERROR IS PLUS OR MINUS 84 PERCENTAGE POINTS.

1% VOTED FOR THE NEW NOSE. 15% VOTED FOR THE OLD, "CLASSIC" NOSE... AND 84% VOTED FOR IMMEDIATELY REPLACING THIS COMIC STRIP WITH "PRINCE VALIANT."

THOSE LATTER VOTES ARE DISQUALIFIED.

THE MASSES HAVE SPOKEN.

THOSE STUPID HORSE-BRAINED MASSES !!

SURGERY

SO! A NEW NOSE JOB BY FORCE, EH ?! COMMANDED BY THE WILL OF THE **PEOPLE**, EH ? THIS IS DEMOCRACY RUN WILD !!

HONKER RECOVERY ROOM

TO HECK WITH DEMOCRACY ! WHAT THIS COUNTRY NEEDS IS A LITTLE **LESS** DEMOCRACY ! LIKE A **MONARCHY** ! LIKE ROYALTY !

"...LIKE PRINCE CHARLES AND DIANA !...WHO, BY THE WAY, JUST VISITED LAST WEEK... AND WHO, IF I MAY BE SO BOLD, COULD BOTH USE A LITTLE NOSE-BOBBING *THEMSELVES,* THANK YOU !!

LIKE HOW I CAME FULL CIRCLE ON THAT ONE ?

HONKER RECOVERY ROOM

≋ SIGH ≋ ... WARP SIX, MR. SULU.

≋ SIGH ≋ ... WHERE TO, SCOTTY ?

≋ SIGH... ≋ WELL ...UH "THE UNTAMED PLANET OF MODERATELY MORAL STENOGRAPHERS."

COME AGAIN ?

WELL **YOU** THINK OF A PLANET, SULU.

THIS JUST ISN'T THE SAME WITHOUT THE CAPTAIN.

CUTTER JOHN.. WHERE ARE YOU ?!

THIS IS YOUR FAULT, SQUID-BAIT.

I CAN'T REMEMBER !

LANIE... I WANT YOU TO MARRY ME.

Bill the Cat OYSTER BAR

MARRY ?

ENOUGH OF THIS FOOLING AROUND... LET'S SETTLE DOWN AND START A FAMILY.

I DON'T WANT TO START A FAMILY !

LANIE...BABY... SUGAR BOO-BOO... HOW LONG HAVE WE BEEN DATING NOW ?

TWENTY MINUTES.

AND MY BIOLOGICAL CLOCK IS TICKING !

WHAT'S WITH STEVE?

REJECTED.

HE PROPOSED AGAIN?

FOURTEENTH THIS YEAR.

HOW'S HE TAKING IT?

LIKE USUAL

I FOUND YOUR EGO IN A PUDDLE BY THE TRASH. I'LL JUST MOP IT UP.

OKAY! SO I WANT SOME TRADITIONAL VALUES IN A WIFE! SO I WANT SOMEONE TO STAY AT HOME AND RAISE A FAMILY! SO I WANT SOMEONE TO WASH MY FEET!... AM I A CRIMINAL?! AM I A SOCIAL LEPER?!

FOR GOODNESS SAKE.. EITHER SEND OFF FOR ONE OF THOSE ASIAN "MAIL-ORDER BRIDES" OR PLEASE HUSH UP!

ASIAN MAIL-ORDER BRI....

WHY DO I FEEL AS IF I'VE JUST CAUSED A TRAIN WRECK?

I LOVE YOU!

DON'T DO IT, STEVE DALLAS! BUYING AN ASIAN MAIL-ORDER WIFE IS SOCIALLY REPUGNANT!!

SHAME! A PURCHASED WIFE! TO LOVE YOU! COOK FOR YOU! PAMPER YOU! WORSHIP YOU... BATHE YOU...

WHICH, OF COURSE, IF VIEWED FROM A STRICTLY NEO-SOCIO-MASCULINE POINT OF VIEW, MIGHT EVEN BE CONSIDERED ALMOST...

...VERY VERY REPUGNANT!

≈WHACK!≈

BLOOM COUNTY BEACON · DECE...

LOCAL LAWYER ANNOUNCES PLAN TO SEND FOR ASIAN MAIL-ORDER WIFE

"WHERE HAVE ALL THE TRADITIONAL DAMES GONE?" ASKS LONELY BACHELOR

STEVE IS TOTALLY OUT OF HIS FAT HEAD. IT'S IMMORAL, OF COURSE... I SENT OPUS OUT TO WARN HIM.

WARN HIM ABOUT WHAT?

"THE MEADOW MORALS SQUAD."

THE WHAT?

"THE MEADOW MORALS SQUAD."

THE WHAT?

WAP! WAP!

SHAME! SHAME! SHAME!

SEE..FIRST I PICK OUT A GIRL FROM THESE PICS... WRITE HER A FEW LETTERS... PROPOSE.. SEND SOME DOUGH TO THE "BRIDE BROKER"...

..AND THEN FLY HER OVER HERE AND WE GET MARRIED. THUS, SHE GETS AMERICA AND I GET LIFELONG DEVOTION AND PAMPERING.

SO. WHADDYA THINK?

I THINK WHITE SLAVERY IS IMMORAL... AND IMMORALITY MAKES MY FEET ITCH!

WHICH, OF COURSE, MAKES ME SECRETLY WISH THAT SEVERAL LOVELY GO-GO DANCERS WOULD MASSAGE THEM ... WHICH, OF COURSE, IS JUST THE TYPICALLY EMBARRASSING MORAL CONTRADICTION I'M ALWAYS CAUGHT IN!

Dear Mail-Order Bride #39,
Hello. My name is Steve. How are things in the Third World? Miserable? So let's get hitched.

I'm sure you are a wonderful person and love men. Unlike American women. And what am I like?...

...Well, to give you a good idea, just think of two simple words...

"...DON JOHNSON."

ACCEPT THE SITUATION... SETTLE DOWN!

NO! LET ME OUT IMMEDIATELY!

BANG! BANG!

"TO EVERYTHING, THERE IS A SEASON... AND TO EVERY PURPOSE, UNDER HEAVEN... A TIME TO LAUGH, A TIME TO CRY, A TIME TO LIVE, A TIME TO DIE--"

NO!

BANG BANG BANG BANG BANG BANG

THE "BANANA JR. 6000" DOES NOT FACE OBSOLESCENCE WITH GREAT POETIC DIGNITY.

OUT! LEMME OUT OR I'LL SPIT!!

FACING FATAL OBSOLESCENCE IS A TRAUMATIC EXPERIENCE FOR A P.C. ...OFTEN INVOLVING THREE DISTINCT PHASES...

DOOMED? I'M DOOMED?

"DENIAL"..

NO WAY! CAN'T BE! IT'S A BIG MISTAKE! THEY MUST'VE MEANT AN I.B.M....

"BARGAINING"...

OH PLEASE, GREAT VIDEO GOD... GIVE ME JUST SIX MORE MONTHS... AND NO MORE HACKING!! I SWEAR! I SWEAR!!

... AND FINALLY... "ACCEPTANCE."

SUDDENLY... LIFE HAS BECOME SO...SO SPECIAL... SO MEANINGFUL.. LISTEN!...THE LOONS!...CAN YOU HEAR THE LOONS?...

TELL YOU WHAT.. BEFORE I THROW YOU OUT, WE'LL GO FOR ONE MORE ROUND OF HACKING... JUST FOR OLD TIMES' SAKE.

OH LET'S! YES! FOR OLD TIMES' SAKE! OH, LET'S **DO**!

WE'LL DAWDLE THROUGH A FEW FILES... TAMPER WITH A FEW PROGRAMS...

CAN WE LAND THE SPACE SHUTTLE ON THE KREMLIN ROOF?

IF YOU LIKE.

CAN WE HOPELESSLY SCRAMBLE WEINBERGER'S FILES?!

YOU! ALWAYS THE SCOUNDREL!

BUT USER FRIENDLY!

NO SCHOOL FOR ME TODAY, DAD. I AM ILL... NAY, SPIRITUALLY **WOUNDED**.

YES, I HAVE BEEN LISTENING TO MY ROCK RECORDS AGAIN... AND HAVING BEEN PUMMELED BY THE OBSCENITIES...THE VIOLENT LYRICS..THE SATANIC IMAGERY... I...I FEEL LIKE GOING OUT TO MURDER AND ASSOCIATE WITH ATHEISTS.

..IN OTHER WORDS, DAD, I SUFFER FROM... FROM... **ROCKINEUMONIA** AND THE **BOOGIE-WOOGIE BLUES**.

SO MUCH FOR THE OL' BOOGIE-WOOGIE BLUES RUSE.

SCHOOL THATAWAY

WHAT'S THAT, BINKLEY?

AN ENVELOPE I FOUND IN BILL THE CAT'S ROOM.

COMPROMISING PICTURES OF JEANE KIRKPATRICK!

THEY'RE ADDRESSED TO... **THE SOVIET EMBASSY**...

HMM...

HMM...

EDITOR'S NOTE ——
THE PRECEDING EXCHANGE WAS AN EXAMPLE OF "FORESHADOWING".. OR, A SUBTLE HINT OF PLOT DEVELOP-MENTS TO COME. A COMMON LITER-ARY DEVICE, IT'S OFTEN USED IN CONTRAST TO ANOTHER, LESS-IMPRESSIVE LITERARY DEVICE..THAT OF "MAKING IT UP AS YOU GO".. WHICH, BY THE WAY, IS A LITERARY DEVICE FREQUENTLY SEEN IN OTHER FEATURES....SUCH AS, SAY, "NANCY." BUT NEVER, **NEVER** HERE.

REMEMBER: "FORESHADOWING"... YOUR CLUE TO QUALITY LITERATURE.

SAY, BILL, WE FOUND THE COMPROMISING PHOTOS OF JEANE KIRKPATRICK THAT YOU WERE ABOUT TO SEND TO THE RUSSIANS.

THERE ISN'T ANY DARK, UGLY SECRET THAT YOU'D LIKE TO TELL US, IS THERE?

NYET!

NYET!

HMM.

HMM.

NYET! NYET! ACKTHPHT!

EDITOR'S NOTE ——
DID EVERYONE CATCH IT? "FORE-SHADOWING"...A SIGN OF VALID, SUBSTANTIVE LITERATURE. AND THIS LITERARY FORM IS AS VALID AS ANY, DESPITE WHAT SOME CRITICS HAVE RECENTLY SAID. LIKE WILLIAM F. BUCKLEY. NOT THAT WE HERE AT "BLOOM COUNTY" ARE INSECURE.. WE'RE **NOT**. AT ALL.

"FORESHADOWING"... A SIGN OF VALID, SUBSTANTIVE LITERATURE.

BUCKLEY IS A WIMPY PUTZ.

HMM... SOMEBODY WITH A RUSSIAN ACCENT JUST CALLED FOR BILL THE CAT. HMM...

WELL?

WELL WHAT?

WHAT DO WE CALL WHAT JUST HAPPENED?

HECK IF I KNOW.

FORE-SHADOWING!

WELL SORRY, BUT I NEVER READ THE "EDITOR'S NOTES"!!

CHRISTMAS TIME... IT'S ALWAYS A... GOOD TIME.

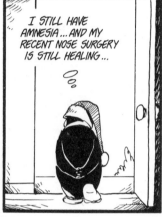

I STILL HAVE AMNESIA... AND MY RECENT NOSE SURGERY IS STILL HEALING...

BUT ON THE WHOLE, IT'S A GOOD TIME HERE IN BLOOM COUNTY... AND EVERYTHING IS...

...CALM.

F.B.I.. A MR. BILL THE CAT IS WANTED FOR SELLING SECRETS TO THE RUSSIANS.

BILL THE CAT... IS A SOVIET SPY?

HE'S BEEN ROMANCING JEANE KIRKPATRICK AND SPONGING HER FOR INFORMATION.

I'M MORTIFIED.

THERE HE GOES DOWN THE HALL!

GIVE IT UP, CAT!!

HE'S FLUSHING HIMSELF DOWN THE COMMODE!

NO VIOLENCE! NO VIOLENCE!

YOU HAVE THE RIGHT TO REMAIN SILENT... IF YOU GIVE UP-- NO DROOLING! ...IF YOU GIVE UP THAT RIGHT, YOUR...

MY LIFE IS SHATTERED.

MILO! THEY'VE ARRESTED BILL THE CAT FOR SELLING SECRETS TO THE RUSSIANS! YEAH! AND THEY'RE RANSACKING THE HOUSE!

LISTEN... I CAN'T GET INVOLVED WITH THIS! I'M ALLERGIC TO SCANDAL! HOW DO WE KEEP THIS OUT OF THE PAPERS? YOU'RE THE EXPERT! YOU'RE A REPORTER! YOU'RE A JOURNAL-- UH...

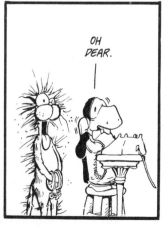

OH DEAR.

The Bloom Beacon

BILL THE CAT: TRAITOR!

THE CAT

GOOD FRIEND

The Bill the Cat —1985— CHRISTMAS CATALOG

FOR Last-Minute SHOPPERS

SANTA BILL

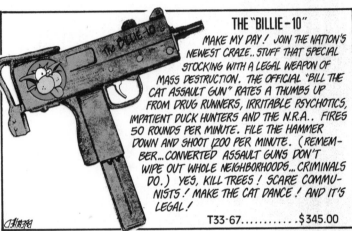

THE "BILLIE-10"

MAKE MY DAY! JOIN THE NATION'S NEWEST CRAZE.. STUFF THAT SPECIAL STOCKING WITH A LEGAL WEAPON OF MASS DESTRUCTION. THE OFFICIAL "BILL THE CAT ASSAULT GUN" RATES A THUMBS UP FROM DRUG RUNNERS, IRRITABLE PSYCHOTICS, IMPATIENT DUCK HUNTERS AND THE N.R.A.. FIRES 50 ROUNDS PER MINUTE. FILE THE HAMMER DOWN AND SHOOT 1200 PER MINUTE. (REMEMBER...CONVERTED ASSAULT GUNS DON'T WIPE OUT WHOLE NEIGHBORHOODS...CRIMINALS DO.) YES, KILL TREES! SCARE COMMUNISTS! MAKE THE CAT DANCE! AND IT'S LEGAL!

T33-67.......... $345.00

KIRKPATRICK PATCH DOLL

SHE'S LOVABLE! SHE'S HUGGABLE! SHE'S A DOLL!... AND SHE'S ALL BILL'S! BUT NOW SHE CAN BE YOURS, TOO! FORMED OF THE HARDEST, COLDEST PLASTIC AND STUFFED FULL WITH THE SOFTEST SHREDDED CLIPPINGS FROM THE "NATIONAL REVIEW", SHE COMES WITH BOTH REPUBLICAN AND DEMOCRATIC BIRTH CERTIFICATES. SQUEEZE HER AND SHE SAYS "U.N. SUCKS EGGS!"

T34-78.......... $49.95

DREAM DATE

PURCHASE AN UNFORGETTABLE EVENING OF ROMANCE AND GOOD WINE WITH EITHER ONE OF OUR THREE FANTASY FELLAS...

SAM SHEPARD

BAD TEETH BUT PRETTY SMART FOR AN ACTOR. OCCASIONALLY LIVES IN SIN WITH JESSICA LANGE, WHO HAS FINE TEETH.
T89-66...... $2000.00

NICK RHODES OF "DURAN DURAN"

SORT OF SHORT AND WEARS LAVENDER LIPSTICK... BUT VERY, VERY HOT.
T78-45.... $2500.00

OPUS

BAD TEETH. SHORT. NO LIPSTICK. WOULD DESPERATELY LIKE TO BE LIVING IN SIN WITH JESSICA LANGE. NEVERTHELESS, HE IS VERY, VERY AVAILABLE.

T65-53....... $9.95

WELL, NOT *THAT* AVAILABLE.

FOR RENT

ORDER FORM

ITEM #	ITEM NAME	SIZE	COLOR	CALIBER	ITEM PRICE	TOTAL PRICE
						TOTAL

IF PURCHASING ASSAULT GUN, FEDERAL LAW REQUIRES FILLING OUT THE AFFIDAVIT BELOW:

☐ I AM A CRIMINAL.   ☐ I AIN'T A CRIMINAL.

NEXT WEEK.. MORE SWELL GIFTS! PLUS BIG CONTEST!

The BILL THE CAT
—1985—
CHRISTMAS CATALOG

FOR THE LAST-MINUTE SHOPPER

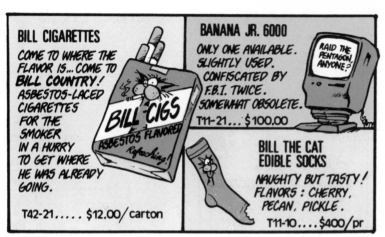

BILL CIGARETTES

COME TO WHERE THE FLAVOR IS...COME TO **BILL COUNTRY!** ASBESTOS-LACED CIGARETTES FOR THE SMOKER IN A HURRY TO GET WHERE HE WAS ALREADY GOING.

T42-21 . . . . . $12.00/carton

BILL-CIGS ASBESTOS FLAVORED *Refreshing!*

BANANA JR. 6000

ONLY ONE AVAILABLE. SLIGHTLY USED. CONFISCATED BY F.B.I. TWICE. SOMEWHAT OBSOLETE.

T11-21 . . . $100.00

RAID THE PENTAGON, ANYONE?

BILL THE CAT EDIBLE SOCKS

NAUGHTY BUT TASTY! FLAVORS : CHERRY, PECAN, PICKLE.

T11-10 . . . . $400/pr

THE REAGAN / GORBACHEV TAPES

A MUST FOR SUMMIT BUFFS! THE ACTUAL CONVERSATIONS BETWEEN THE TWO SUPER-POWER BIGGIES, SECRETLY RECORDED DURING THEIR TEATIME TALKS IN GENEVA LAST MONTH. AN EXCERPT:

MRS. REAGAN —"HELLO."
MRS. GORBACHEV — "HELLO."
MRS. REAGAN — "NICE HAT."
MRS. GORBACHEV— "THANKS."
MRS. REAGAN — "SO, DOES YOUR MIKHAIL SNORE ?" (etc...)

T78-80 . . . . . $7000.00

HELD OVER!

DREAM DATE WITH OPUS !!

CHOICE EVENINGS **STILL** AVAILABLE ! QUICK ! WRITE FOR RESERVATIONS NOW ! HURRY ! QUICK ! THEY'RE GOING FAST !

$1.25
T65-53 . . . . $9.98

I'M A PERFECT GENTLEMAN... TRULY I AM... NO HICKIES... I PROMISE... HELLO ?

FOR RENT CHEAP

ORDER FORM

ITEM	#	SIZE	COLOR	GLOVE SIZE	NOSE SIZE	PRICE
						TOTAL

EASY TERMS— TAKE 60 DAYS TO PAY. EXCEPT FOR "DREAM DATE WITH OPUS."... CASH UP FRONT FOR THAT.

BIG CONTEST
DRAW BILL ...AND WIN BILL .!!

DRAW, ON A POSTCARD ONLY... BILL THE CAT IN A SCENE REFLECTING THE JOYOUS HOLIDAY SEASON... (FOR INSTANCE, SPITTING EGGNOG ON AN ELF)

PRIZES WILL BE AWARDED FOR BOTH THE BEST AND AND THE ABSOLUTE **WORST** SKETCH ...

WINNING ENTRIES WILL BE SHOWN HERE FEBRUARY 9TH.

USE BLACK INK...ON A POSTCARD ONLY... AND SEND TO:

BILL'S BIG CONTEST
P.O. BOX 30067
ALBUQUERQUE, N.M. 87190-0067

THE PRIZE : STUFFED BILL DOLLS

STUFFED W/ FOAM FROM OLD "GARFIELD" DOLL

THE ONLY TWO IN EXISTENCE... AND GETTING MORE VALUABLE BY THE MICRO-SECOND.

SO, BILL THE CAT... THIS NATION'S LATEST TRAITOROUS SPY, IS BEHIND BARS.

BUT THE QUESTION REMAINS... WHO WAS HIS CONNECTION? WHO WAS HE IN CAHOOTS WITH? WHO ELSE OUT THERE IS A SHAMEFUL, RED SWINE?

WE HAVE A PHOTO OF A POSSIBLE, UNIDENTIFIED SUSPECT...

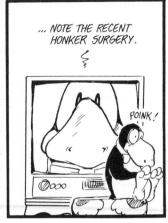

... NOTE THE RECENT HONKER SURGERY.

POINK!

SO THE QUESTION REMAINS... JUST WHAT IS THE CONNECTION BETWEEN THE TRAITOROUS BILL THE CAT AND THIS MYSTERIOUS "MISTER BIG NOSE"?

NONE! ALMOST NONE!

DID THEY KNOW EACH OTHER?

BARELY... JUST BARELY!

WERE THEY FRIENDS?

PASSING ACQUAINTANCES!

"THEY WERE LIKE BROTHERS," SAID ATTORNEY STEVE DALLAS.

HOLY GALLOPING GORBACHEVS!!

I'M IMPLICATED! I'VE BEEN LINKED WITH THE TRAITOROUS BILL THE CAT!! WHAT WILL BECOME OF ME?!

DOESN'T MATTER. NOTHING MATTERS. WE ARE ALL GOING TO BE SMASHED BY HALLEY'S COMET. THERE'S NO FUTURE.

MEANING, ESSENTIALLY, THAT YOU WILL NEVER HAVE THAT OPPORTUNITY TO PLAY SERIOUS SNUGGLEBUNNIES WITH DIANE SAWYER.

WHAT AN UTTERLY ABOMINABLE DISAPPOINTMENT.

"F.B.I.". WE WANT A MISTER P. OPUS FOR QUESTIONING IN THE BILL THE CAT AFFAIR.

BLOOM BOARDING HOUSE

NO LICE

MAY WE COME IN?

UH... ONE MOMENT PLEASE...

BLOOM BOARDING HOUSE

NO LICE

I WON'T GO TO PRISON!! PRISON GIVES ME PIMPLES!! I'LL FIGHT! GO ON! LET THE NAZIS IN! I'M READY! YA! YA! YA!

YOU'LL PARDON US IF THERE'S A LITTLE PANDEMONIUM IN THE POTTY...

BLOOM BOARDING HOUSE

NO LICE

AWRIGHT.. WHEN DID YA START SELLING SECRETS WITH YER FRIEND BILL THE CAT?

N-NEVER! I-I SWEAR!

LOOK.. CONFESS TO EVERYTHING AND YOU'LL WALK OUT OF HERE FREE AND BE SUCKING HERRING LIVERS WITHIN THE HOUR.

REALLY?

I'M GUILTY! I DID EVERYTHING! GUILTY! I CONFESS! THAT'S ME... MR. GUILTY!

BOOK HIM.

YER GONNA FRY.

OH, I AM SO GULLIBLE!!

BONK BONK

GREAT. TWO ACCUSED RED SPIES FOR CLIENTS. MY CAREER IS IN THE TOILET.

HAVEN'T YOU PEOPLE BEEN TO THE MOVIES LATELY? COMMIES AREN'T FASHIONABLE, GUYS... IN FACT, PERSONALLY, I'D LIKE TO SEE BOTH OF YOU STRUNG UP AND GUTTED LIKE A COUPLE OF ROTTEN TUNA!!

..BUT YOU WON'T BE. 'CAUSE I'M DEFENDING YOU. AND ALL MY INFINITE POWERS ARE AT YOUR DISPOSAL...

ZZZ.

THPTH!

SOMEBODY GET ME JOYCE DAVENPORT.

I'VE CALLED THIS NEWS CONFERENCE TO ANNOUNCE THAT MY CLIENT HERE, MR. OPUS, IS COMPLETELY INNOCENT OF BEING A FILTHY COMMUNIST SPY...

INNOCENT

FURTHERMORE...

STEVE... THERE'S A MAN OVER THERE IN A "ROCKY IV" SHIRT LOOKING VERY SUSPICIOUS...

NOCENT

U.S.A.! U.S.A.!

HE'S GOT A GUN!!

YOW!

INNOCENT

THE FINAL PANEL OF THIS SEQUENCE HAS BEEN CENSORED BY THE FEDERAL COMICS COUNCIL FOR REASONS OF SHOCKING AND GRATUITOUS VIOLENCE. WE ARE, HOWEVER, ALLOWED TO DESCRIBE THE ACTION: SUFFICE TO SAY THERE ARE BULLETS, FEATHERS, BODY PARTS AND PENGUIN PLASMA FLYING AROUND ALL HIGGLEDY-PIGGLEDY.

TRULY. IT'S JUST AWFUL.

OPUS HAS BEEN SHOT BY A CRAZED ASSASSIN!! HE'S IN A COMA!!

SOME TEEN-AGER SAT THROUGH 20 STRAIGHT HOURS OF RECENT SYLVESTER STALLONE MOVIES, WENT INTO ANTI-SOVIET HYSTERICS AND THEN SHOT OPUS'...UH... HIS...

WHAT? HE SHOT HIS WHAT?!

NOW DON'T GET MAD...

..HIS NOSE?!

..CLEAN OFF. THEY'VE CALLED A COSMETIC SURGEON.

211

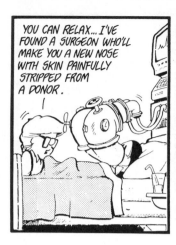

YOU CAN RELAX... I'VE FOUND A SURGEON WHO'LL MAKE YOU A NEW NOSE WITH SKIN PAINFULLY STRIPPED FROM A DONOR.

MMPH... SNORT MM...MMPH.?

WHAT? WHO'S THE DONOR? WHY, JUST A CHEERFUL VOLUNTEER...

NOW YOU GUYS SAY WE'RE GOIN' TO A "SKIN PARTY," RIGHT?

OOF...

ARRESTED FOR SPYING... SHOT BY A "RAMBO"-CRAZED LUNATIC... HOOKED UP TO A RIDICULOUS FAKE HONKER... AND THEN I RECEIVED A NEW NOSE FROM THE SKIN OF STEVE DALLAS' THIGH.

AND NOW STANDING HERE LIKE A DINK WITH MY HONKER IN SWADDLING BANDAGES...

ONLY ONE THING COMES TO MIND...

DÉJÀ VU.

The Bloom Beacon

BILL THE CAT TRIAL STARTS TODAY

"THPFFT" SAYS CAT

"TOTALLY INNOCENT" SAYS LAWYER

SPY TRIALS ALWAYS MAKE ME SO NERVOUS..

RELAX. STEVE IS DEFENDING HIM.

BILL THE CAT AND STEVE DALLAS...

TRULY... THE DYNAMIC DUO...

SAY, YOU DON'T SUPPOSE THE "JURY BOX" IS ANYTHING LIKE A "LITTER BOX," DO YOU?

SHUT UP. I DON'T TALK TO COMMUNISTS.

AWRIGHT... NOW, WHEN THE PROSECUTOR ASKS YOU IF YOU'RE A COMMIE SPY, ANSWER "LORD, NO! I LOVE AMERICA, APPLE PIE AND LEE IACOCCA!"

CAN YOU SAY THAT? TRY IT... "LORD, NO..." GO ON...

L.... LO....

THAT'S RIGHT...

..LONG LIVE THE GLORIOUS STRUGGLE AGAINST CAPITALIST OPPRESSMMPH!

THAT'S NOT RIGHT.

LAUGHABLE! YES, YOUR HONOR... IT'S LAUGHABLE TO EVEN **THINK** THAT MY CLIENT IS A COMMUNIST. IN FACT, HE IS AN IMPECCABLY **MORAL** CITIZEN.

THE PROSECUTION WOULD LIKE TO SUBMIT A PHOTO OF THE DEFENDANT AT A MOSCOW NUDIST CAMP IN THE SPRING OF 1982.

MY CAREER IS IN THE TOILET.

THPTH.

OKAY, GENTLEMEN... THIS TRIAL IS DRAGGING. LET'S SEE A LITTLE DEALING HERE.

YOUR HONOR, ESPIONAGE IS A SERIOUS CRIME. THE PEOPLE WON'T SETTLE FOR LESS THAN "GUILTY OF ANTI-STATE ACTIVITIES."

HA! WHAT A CROCK! MY CLIENT IS GUILTY OF HIGH TREASON. YOU KNOW IT. I KNOW IT. SO LET'S SEE JUSTICE DONE AND SEND HIM TO THE CHAIR. NOW, LET'S BLOW THIS DUMP AND GO FOR PIZZA.

NOW **THAT** WAS PLEA BARGAINING.

YEAH! YEAH! YEAH!

THUS, MR. CAT, YOUR LAWYER HAVING PLEA BARGAINED YOU INTO THE ELECTRIC CHAIR, I NOW SENTENCE YOU TO DIE ON —

HE'S INNOCENT! I'M A SURPRISE WITNESS WITH A SHOCKING ALIBI!!

BILL WAS WITH ME THE WHOLE TIME! YES! WITH ME!... A **LOOSE** MYSTERY WOMAN!! LIVING IN SIN! MY REPUTATION IS RUINED! BUT I HAD TO COME FORWARD! I LOVE HIM! I...I..

YOU'RE NOT BUYING A SMIDGEN OF THIS, ARE YOU?

HE MUST'VE NOTICED MY ADAM'S APPLE!!

AS I WAS SAYING...

MILO! DO YOU REALIZE BILL THE CAT HAS BEEN SENTENCED TO DEATH?! HE'S GONNA DIE! DIE!!

BOBBLE BOBBLE BOBBLE

HAPPENS TO THE BEST OF US EVENTUALLY, BINKLEY.

OH, WHAT MUST HE BE GOING THROUGH RIGHT NOW?

PROBABLY AN INITIAL FITTING...

FITTING?

CAN YOU... YOU KNOW, STRETCH UP A BIT?

214

I MISS CUTTER JOHN.

IT'S ABOUT TIME OPUS SNAPPED OUT OF HIS AMNESIA AND TOLD US WHAT HAPPENED ON THEIR ILL-FATED BALLOON TRIP.

IT'LL PROBABLY TAKE SOME SORT OF JOLT TO JOG HIS MEMORY.

HOW ABOUT A BASEBALL BAT TO THE HEAD?

NO! NO! IT HAS TO BE MENTAL... SOME AWFUL, TRAUMATIC, JOLTING SHOCK TO HIS SENSES...

LIKE WHAT?

DIANE SAWYER MARRIED EDDIE MURPHY TODAY...

AAAIGH!

WHAT HAPPENED?

HE HEARD AN ERRONEOUS REPORT THAT DIANE SAWYER HAD MARRIED. HE'S HAD A TERRIBLE SHOCK.

OPUS! TALK TO US! HAVE YOU BEEN JOLTED OUT OF YOUR AMNESIA? WHAT DO YOU REMEMBER?

TELL US ABOUT YOUR ADVENTURE!

I... I... UH...

TOTO?

WRONG ADVENTURE!

I...I REMEMBER EVERYTHING NOW... ME AND CUTTER JOHN... WE SPLASHED DOWN SOMEWHERE IN THE ATLANTIC...

BUT WE DIDN'T PANIC... WE HAD PROFESSIONAL EMERGENCY EQUIPMENT... AND, OF COURSE, I HAD PACKED EXCELLENT EMERGENCY PROVISIONS...

... CANNED MILK, CANNED HAM, CANNED PEACHES, CANNED QUICHE...

WHERE'S THE CAN OPENER?

THE WHAT?

RONCO FLOAT-A-MATIC WHEELCHAIR

FOR THE FIRST FEW DAYS, THE TERRIBLE REALITY OF OUR PLIGHT BEGAN TO STRAIN OUR FORMERLY CLOSE RELATIONSHIP...

ANY NIBBLES, PINK-BRAIN?

RONCO FLOAT-A-MATIC WHEELCHAIR

NO..BUT MAY I AGAIN OFFER ANOTHER PROFOUND APOLOGY FOR MY INEXPLICABLE OVERSIGHT IN FORGETTING THE STUPID CAN OPENER!

SHARKS! COME N' GET IT! ↓ ↓ BIG TASTY BAIT

..WE DRIFTED FOR DAYS... WEEKS.. DECADES... I LOST TRACK ...

WE HAD NO FOOD.. NO WATER... BUT, THANK GOD, WE DID HAVE ONE THING ...

... WE HAD EACH OTHER.

WELL. YOU'RE LOOKING GROSS THIS MORNING.

SO PICK ME UP SOME CREAM RINSE, STUBBLE FACE!

"OH, THE HEAT! OFTEN I HAD PROLONGED FEVER DREAMS.."

IT'S.. CHRISTMAS! SNOW... I SEE SNOW... COOL, WONDERFUL SNOW...

AND THERE...THERE'S CYBILL SHEPHERD... SHE'S WEARING ONLY... CHRISTMAS STOCKINGS... I... I'M RUBBING ICE ON HER SHOULDERS.. ..ON HER NECK... ON ...

ON WHAT?!

ON, DONNER! ON, BLITZEN!...

EVENTUALLY, SAVAGE BOREDOM SET IN..

SAYS HERE THAT JANE PAULEY IS PREGNANT AGAIN.

I KNOW!

IN FACT, YOU'VE TOLD ME NINE TIMES! IN FACT, YOU'VE READ THAT MAGAZINE NINE TIMES! IN FACT, I DON'T WANT TO HEAR ABOUT JANE PAULEY'S NEW BABY EVEN ONE MORE TIME!!

NATIONAL ENQUIRER

NATIONAL ENQUIRER

THE FATHER IS A SPACE ALIEN.

I KNOW!!

LAND!! WE'RE SAVED! SNATCHED FROM THE JAWS OF FATE!!

FULL AHEAD!

AN ISLAND! IT'S AN ISLAND! IT'S A BIG ISLAND! IT'S... IT'S...

SKIPPER?.. PROFESSOR?... MR. AND MRS. HOWELL?

IT'S GILLIGAN'S ISLAND.

FULL ASTERN!!

SPLASH SPLASH SPLASH

EXCUSE ME. WHAT ISLAND IS THIS?

"THE ISLAND OF PEOPLE WHO REALIZE THAT 'MIAMI VICE' IS GARBAGE."

LOOKIT THIS EPISODE... HERE'S WHATSHISNAME...THE WHITE GUY WITH THE CHEST... HE WALKS UP TO SOME GIRL WHO JUST STOLE HIS GUN AND SAYS TO HER...GET READY FOR THIS – HE SAYS, "HEY... MAJOR UNCOOL."

THAT'S DIALOGUE? HA! IT'S GARBAGE. STYLIZED GARBAGE! GARBAGE! GARBAGE! GARBAGE!

BOY! IMAGINE IF THESE PEOPLE HAD TO LIVE UNPROTECTED AMONG THE REST OF US WHO KNOW BETTER!

HEY.. MAJOR UNCOOL.

AND WHAT STRANGE LAND IS THIS?

"THE LAND OF RADICAL FEMINISTS WHO SECRETLY DIG BEEFCAKE."

WE...WE CAN'T HELP OURSELVES.. MEN ARE LOATHSOME..BUT WHEN WE SEE SYLVESTER STALLONE'S BODY...WE'RE OVERCOME WITH...WITH...

..ANIMALISTIC LASCIVIOUSNESS! PEPPERED HEAVILY WITH OVERWHELMING GUILT!!

YES...I GET THE SAME FEELINGS FOR GLORIA STEINEM.

LEAVE US IN OUR SHAME.

BOY GEORGE! WHY, THIS MUST BE THE--

"THE FORGOTTEN ISLAND OF EFFEMINATE POP STARS."

BANISHED! ALL OF US! BANISHED FROM WORLD ATTENTION! PRINCE...MICHAEL JACKSON...ELTON JOHN...ME... SWEPT OUT THE DOOR LIKE DISCARDED LINGERIE!

IT'S SPRINGSTEEN'S FAULT, OF COURSE...WITH THOSE AWFUL LEVI'S AND WORK SHIRTS...THAT MACHO BOY COULD USE SOME EYESHADOW!

RIGHT. I'M OUTTA HERE.

DARN IT! WIMPS WERE VERY IN, ONCE!

LOVELY. NO HABITABLE ISLANDS. WE'RE DOOMED.

HOLD IT. WHY AREN'T I SEASICK ANYMORE?

WE'RE THIRTY FEET IN THE AIR..

HOLY MACKEREL! I DO BELIEVE IT'S....IT'S... YES!

AHOY CALYPSO! VIVA COUSTEAU!

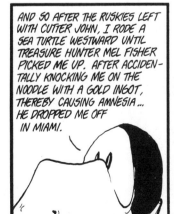

221

The Official Results of
BILL'S BIG ART CONTEST

GRAND PRIZES: BILL DOLLS

—NO— GOOD HOUSEKEEPING SEAL OF APPROVAL

THE 27,366 DRAWINGS WE RECEIVED WERE BROKEN DOWN INTO THE FOLLOWING THEMES...

JUDGE

ENTRIES

BILL DRUNK	6%
BILL ELECTROCUTED	3%
BILL WITH FIREARMS	4%
BILL EXPOSING HIMSELF	2%
BILL IMPALED ON XMAS TREE	9%
BILL EATING GARFIELD	1%
GARFIELD EATING BILL	1%
SCATOLOGICAL THEMES	5%
SEXUAL THEMES	4%
BILL SPITTING HAIRBALLS AT BROOKE SHIELDS	11%
— AT GEORGE MICHAEL OF "WHAM!"	15%
— AT DON JOHNSON'S CHEST	12%
— AT ANY PART OF GEORGE BUSH	23%
OTHER	4%

HONORABLE MENTION "BEST"

"BILL STUFFS A CHRISTMAS TURKEY"
BY SUSANNA CROSBY OF LA JOLLA, CALIFORNIA.

JUDGES: "WELL DONE. SENSITIVE...BUT NOT OVERBEARING. WE WERE DEEPLY MOVED."

HONORABLE MENTION "WORST"

"BILL — A TREE STAND"
BY RICHARD LANDESMAN OF COLCHESTER, VT.

JUDGES: "SICKENING. WARPED. MR. LANDESMAN HAS OBVIOUSLY BEEN LISTENING TO HEAVY METAL ROCK MUSIC."

THWAP!
HIC!
—HIC!

← WORST

"BILL AT THE WHITE HOUSE CHRISTMAS PARTY"
BY ROBERT HOCH OF WHITE PLAINS, N.Y.

JUDGES: "BREATHTAKING IN ITS TASTELESSNESS. THE PRESIDENT OF THE WORLD'S MOST POWERFUL AND MORAL NATION DESERVES MORE RESPECT THAN THIS. MONUMENTALLY INEXCUSABLE. THE ARTIST WINS A BILL DOLL."

GRAND PRIZE WINNERS

BEST →

"UNTITLED"
BY MISS NICOLE TOWNLEY OF PUEBLO, CO.

JUDGES: "SUPERBLY MINIMALIST! SPARSE IN HER USE OF LINE AND FORM, MS. TOWNLEY — ALREADY A MATURE ABSTRACT EXPRESSIONIST AT AGE FIVE, HAS BRILLIANTLY CAPTURED THE MAGIC...THE GLORY...THE WONDER OF A CAT NAMED BILL."

BILL

POSSIBLY AN ELF. OR A BUG. OR "PRINCE"